I0886612

THE RESOURCE ROOM

The Resource Room

A GUIDE FOR SPECIAL EDUCATORS

Barry E. McNamara

STATE UNIVERSITY OF NEW YORK PRESS

Published by
State University of New York Press, Albany

Printed in the United States of America

For information, address the State University of New York Press, 90 State Street, Suite 700, Albany, NY 12207

Library of Congress Cataloging-in-Publication Data

McNamara, Barry E., 1949–
The resource room: a guide for special educators / Barry E. McNamara.
p. cm.
Includes index.
ISBN 0-88706-983-5. ISBN 0-88706-984-3 (pbk.)
1. Resource programs (Education) 2. Special education.
I. Title.
LB1028.8.M37 1989
371.9—dc19 88-20086
CIP

10 9 8 7 6 5 4 3 2 1

To Fran, Tracy, and Melissa

Contents

Acknowledgments

As a former resource room teacher I have always been excited about the possibilities that existed for this service delivery model. This stimulating, sometimes overwhelming, position allows teachers to have an impact on students, parents, colleagues, and the entire school program. Over the years I have had many opportunities to discuss these possibilities with resource room teachers, regular educators, and students who attend the resource room. These experiences have provided me with the impetus for writing this textbook, and for this I acknowledge their contributions. One individual in particular has provided me with innumerable opportunities in the "real world" of the school: Dr. L. Jay Lev, assistant superintendent, Harborfield Central School District, Greenlawn, New York. Dr. Vincent Aniello, director of special education, Parsippany-Troy Hills School District, Parsippany, New Jersey, has also been instrumental in enabling me to have access to a variety of educational settings that have influenced my thinking on the resource room — in particular, the role of communication between regular and special educators.

Lois Patton, editor in chief of State University of New York Press, has been generous with her time and expertise and has provided support and encouragement. Her involvement and the helpful suggestions of the field reviewers have clearly strengthened this textbook.

I have been blessed with a wonderful family. They have always been enthusiastic and supportive of anything that I have undertaken, and this book was no different. Their encouragement from the initial prospectus to the final chapter enabled me to stay on task. Their excitement and concern for my efforts was always apparent. It is for this — and other reasons too numerous to mention — that I dedicate this work with love and appreciation to my wife, Fran, and our daughters, Melissa and Tracy.

1

The Resource Room: An Introduction

HISTORICAL PERSPECTIVE

The special educator who is assigned to a resource room and the regular educator whose students attend the resource room are probably not concerned about historical roots of these programs. Clearly, their needs are more immediate. However, it appears appropriate and necessary to address this issue in a textbook of this nature. The resource room movement is not new, nor are there universally accepted guidelines for teachers in these programs. The practitioner should be aware of the development of this service delivery model in order to better appreciate the nature of the current practices associated with it.

What is the Special Education Resource Room?

Physically, the resource room is a classroom where students come for part of their instructional day to receive special education services.

However, it is more than just a physical space. It is a concept that calls our attention to the fact that students with special educational needs can benefit from regular classroom placement. The placement of a special education student in a resource room program still gives the student considerable time in the regular classroom. And although most states have guidelines for the amount of time to be spent in the resource room, the important point is not the specified time, but rather the notion that this placement is significantly different from the special education self-contained classroom. The student who is placed in a self-contained class spends most of the instructional day in this setting and receives his or her primary instruction from the special education teacher. By contrast, the student who is placed in a resource room spends no more than half of the day in the resource room and receives supplemental instruction from the special education teacher. The primary instruction takes place in the regular classroom setting. The resource room teacher provides the student with the ways and means to succeed in the regular classroom. This arrangement represents a markedly different way of providing services to students with special educational needs and has resulted in some confusion for special and regular educators alike.

Theoretical Rationale

Although many attribute the popularity of the resource room to the mainstreaming* movement, its origins appear to have a stronger base. Early proponents of the resource room model pointed to the increasing uneasiness with the self-contained special classes for educable mentally retarded students. Dunn (1968), in his now classic article, questioned the justification of placing mildly disabled students in self-contained classes. He was not alone in his concern. Readers interested in investigating the many issues raised can peruse the large body of literature on the efficacy of special education self-contained classes (see Pertsh, 1936; Shattuck, 1946; Johnson, 1962; Dunn, 1968; MacMillan, 1971; Van Etten and Adamson, 1973). Essentially, the placement of students in self-contained classes could not be supported by empirical evidence. As Sabatino (1972) suggested, our justification for such placements may have been "mere rationalization" (p. 335).

If the self-contained classroom was no longer viewed as an acceptable alternative to regular education for mildly disabled students, how could special education services be provided to them? What appeared

* Mainstreaming can be defined as any time a disabled student is educated with his or her nondisabled peer. See Blankenship and Lilly (1981) for further information.

necessary was a service delivery model that allowed disabled students to be educated with their nondisabled peers to the maximum extent possible and at the same time to receive special education in areas of need. Hence the development and implementation of the resource room model.

There is little doubt that resource room programs gained impetus from the mainstreaming movement and the placement of students in the "least restrictive environment (LRE)."* However, it is important to be aware that special education resource room programs were developed on the basis of instructional need, not by legislative or administrative dictates. And they are currently the most frequently used form of special education placement (Friend and McNutt, 1984).

Early Programs

The resource room program is not new to special education. Students with visual impairments were served by resource room teachers as far back as the 1930s (Wiederholt, Hammill, and Brown, 1983). However, its utility for students with mild disabilities, such as those with educable mental retardation, the mildly emotionally disturbed, and the learning disabled, was not proposed until the late 1960s or early 1970s. One of the early programs was developed by Roger Reger (1969) of the Board of Cooperative Educational Services, First Supervisory District, Erie County, New York. Reger noted that an underlying principle of the program was that the resource room teacher does not establish the student's program and expect the school to modify the curriculum. Rather, the resource room teacher must work closely with the regular classroom teacher so that all activities of the resource room teacher revolve around the regular classroom's teacher's program. Reger also was clear in his proposal that the resource room teacher work with teachers as well as with students. He viewed the program as "something between a special class program and a program where little or no assistance beyond the 'regular' program is available" (p. 7).

Reger's optimism about this model was shared by others in the Symposium on the Resource Room Model in Special Education, published in the *Journal of Special Education* (Hammill, 1972, pp. 350-351). In that issue Hammill discusses a number of advantages of this placement alternative. (Note that his remarks are directed to both

---

* LRE refers to the establishment of procedures to ensure that to the maximum extent appropriate disabled students are educated with students who are not disabled. This does not mean that all disabled students are placed in regular settings, only those for whom such placement is appropriate.

categorical and noncategorical resource rooms, both of which will be discussed shortly.) The advantages are as follows:

1. Pupils can benefit from specific resource room training while remaining integrated with their friends and age-mates in school.
2. Pupils have the advantages of a total remedial program which is prepared by the resource teacher but which may be implemented in cooperation with the regular class teacher.
3. Resource rooms are less expensive to operate than tutoring, remedial reading, and special class programs for the handicapped.
4. Resource rooms have a greater multiplier effect than the present system: that is, more children can be served under the resource room arrangement.
5. Since the resource teacher is assigned to a particular school, he or she is less likely than the school psychologist, the remedial reading therapist, the speech correctionist, or other itinerant staff to be viewed as an "outsider" by the other teachers in the school.
6. Since young children with mild, though developing, problems can be accommodated, later severe disorders can be prevented.
7. Since disability diagnoses are not necessary for placement purposes, pupils are not labeled in any way as handicapped.
8. Since labeling and segregation are avoided, the stigma invariably associated with receiving special attention is minimized.
9. Since most elementary schools are large enough to accommodare one or more resource rooms, pupils can receive help in their neighborhood school; this arrangement eliminates or minimizes the necessity for busing "handicapped" children across the town or county to a school housing an "appropriately labeled" class or resource room.
10. Pupils are given flexible scheduling in that remediation can be applied entirely in their classrooms by the regular teacher with some resource teacher support or in the resource room on an as-needed basis; in addition, the scheduling can be quickly altered to meet the changing situations and individual needs of the children.
11. Since placement in the resource room is an individual school matter, involving the principal, the teachers, and the parents, no appreciable time lapse need occur between the teacher's referral and the initiation of special service for the child.
12. Under this alternative, medical and psychological workups are done on a school request basis rather than on a screening-for-placement basis; thus the school psychologist is freed to do the work he or she was trained to do, instead of being relegated to the role of psychometrician.

13. Since the resource room will absorb most of the "handicapped" children in the schools, the special classes will increasingly become instructional settings for the "truly" handicapped pupils, that is, the children for whom the classes were originally intended.

Obviously, programs will vary depending upon state and local educational agency guidelines, and the advantages noted above may not apply across the board to all resource room programs. What is clear, however, is that leaders in the field of special education were rethinking the ways in which special students were served. Sabatino (1972), although somewhat more cautious, still felt strongly about the possibilities that existed with this model when he suggested that resource room programs may lead to a breakthrough in education for mildly disabled students.

Current Status

To be sure, after more than a decade since the Symposium on the Resource Room Model in Special Education (1972), the resource room program has dramatically changed the way in which we provide educational services to mildly disabled students. It has allowed disabled students to be integrated with their nondisabled peers; it has provided many regular classroom teachers with the methods and materials to enable them to teach disabled students in their classroom; and it has forced special educators to be more accountable to the "regular curriculum." And yet, there is much that needs to be done if the resource room is to reach its potential. In 1969, Reger listed some potential problems that would interfere with the success of the resource room program:

1. Allowing the program to become vague so that those involved do not know what is expected of them or what the program is supposed to accomplish.
2. Expecting too much from the program and then becoming disillusioned. The resource room program, any more than the special class programs, will *not* make all children "normal" and will *not* eliminate all problems of most of the children enrolled.
3. Assuming that the resource room program is a total substitute for the special class programs, and thus placing children who should not be placed.
4. Noninvolvement of building principals.
5. Lack of communication and understanding of the program by other teachers in the buildings where the programs are housed.

6. Use of inappropriate physical facilities.

These cautions are as appropriate now as they were almost twenty years ago. Many of them are being violated at this point in time. Add to this list the lack of competent teachers trained in resource rooms on both the elementary and secondary levels and the regular classroom teachers' perceptions of the job of a resource room teacher as being fairly easy, and there is little doubt that the potential of the model has yet to be fulfilled. It appears that the special education resource room is in a critical point of development. In order for it to continue to be viewed as a viable placement alternative, programs need to be developed and implemented in a manner consistent with the optimism of the early proponents of the model and current research findings.

TYPES OF RESOURCE ROOMS

There are three types of resource room programs used in special education: (1) categorical; (2) cross-categorical (or multicategorical); and (3) noncategorical. This division is based upon the particular classification scheme employed by the state or local school district; it does not dictate the practices undertaken in each setting. A nationwide survey of resource room programs (Friend and McNutt, 1984) indicated that 38 states employed several types of programs, the most frequently cited (N = 19) being a combination of categorical and cross-categorical (multicategorical) programs. Of those states employing only one type of resource room program, 80 percent used a categorical approach. A noncategorical resource room program was viewed as an option by only 6 states surveyed. These three types of programs are described below.

Categorical Resource Room Programs

The categorical resource room is one in which special education students are placed on the basis of their specific classification: learning disability, mental retardation, emotional disturbance. A school district using this type of program may have a number of resource rooms in operation, but in each of these special education settings the students would be selected for placement solely on the basis of their classification. Therefore, there might be a resource room on the middle school level for students with learning disabilities, one for students who are emotionally disturbed (or behavior disordered), and still another for those students who are classified as educable mentally retarded. The rationale for such an approach is that there are distinct, nonoverlapping special education categories and that the students within each of these categories have more in common with each other than they do with other students — the disabled and nondisabled. Moreover, it appears that, historically, certain populations (those with mental retardation and emotional disturbance) have been provided with special education services in a more restricted environment (self-contained classes), and the learning disabled population has been provided, for the most part, with resource room programs. This arrangement is probably due more to the propitious timing of the movement toward the least restrictive environment brought about by the Education of All the Handicapped Children's Act (P.L. 94-142) and the emergence of the field of learning disabilities than to issues related to the effectiveness of special education placements. Over time, it appears that placement decisions were based on the classification (learning disabled = resource room; mentally retarded = self-contained; emotionally disturbed = self-contained) rather than the individual needs of the student. In one survey (Suffolk County, N.Y., BOCES 2, 1986) over 86 percent of the students attending resource room programs were classified as learning disabled. At least for this population, the resource room appears to be the placement of choice.

Cross-Categorical Resource Room Programs

In a cross-categorical (multicategorical) resource room program, students are placed on the basis of their specific needs rather than on their particular classification. It would not be unusual in this type of arrangement to have students who are classified as learning disabled, mentally retarded, or emotionally disturbed placed in the same resource room. Those who employ this approach assume that the classification alone does not enable the resource room teacher to develop appropriate educational programs. Other variables, such as academic, social, physical, and behavioral needs, must also be considered for effective programming. These variables make it conceivable (if not predictable) that students whose classifications are different have special needs that are very much alike. Therefore, a school district employing this type of resource room program may have four resource rooms on the primary level and four more on the intermediate level with students who are classified as learning disabled, mentally retarded, and emotionally disturbed in each of these settings, but whose educational and emotional needs are somewhat similar.

Noncategorical Resource Room Programs

Theoretically, this type of program may not be viewed strictly as a special education resource room in that the students are not classified in any of the special education categories. However, there are states and local school districts that employ this type of program and typically do so with a certified special education teacher. The rationale is quite simple — there are students who are in need of assistance but who may not be eligible for special education services. Often, these "at risk" students are receiving resource room services as a "trial" to see if they need to be classified in order to receive additional special education services. A more pragmatic rationale is employed by certain school districts that have great financial resources and that will provide these services without classifying students (and obviously not receiving federal and state reimbursements). Although this approach is typically viewed as being somewhat altruistic, it appears that there are certain "rights" associated with the classification status that may benefit students and their parents. However, all of this must be balanced by the negative aspects of "labeling."

Comparison of Programs

A discussion of the viability of each of the programs noted above must be viewed within the context of the ongoing debate over the effectiveness of special education practices regarding the classification of students. Simply stated, the issues deal with the utility of placing students into specific special education categories such as learning disabled, mentally retarded, emotionally disturbed, and so forth (Glass, 1983; Ysseldyke and Algozzine, 1983). Over a decade ago, Hallahan and Kauffman (1976) noted the commonalities that existed among students with mild to moderate disabilities who were classified as learning disabled, educable mentally retarded, and emotionally disturbed. Their research indicated that when we look at IQ scores, patterns of ability (even development versus uneven development), social and emotional development (maladaptive versus adaptive), and academic achievement (underachieving versus overachieving), these three groups have more characteristics that were similar than dissimilar. More recently the issue has been brought into clearer focus by Reynolds, Wang, and Walberg (1987), who suggest that there is little evidence to support our current categorical system and strongly admonish special educators to "hold themselves accountable to research findings" (p. 393). For administrators who are responsible for resource room programs the charge is clear: the provision of services on a cross-categorical (multicategorical) basis appears to be the most efficacious; therefore, current school programs should make this provision.

Whether or not to provide services in the form of a noncategorical basis is another issue. Since current funding practices do not allow support for such programs, it seems as if only financially secure school districts can provide these services. However, this situation may change given the impetus of Assistant Secretary Will's Regular Education Initiative (1986), by which she calls for a change in our special education delivery of services so that students with learning problems can be served even if they do not meet the current eligibility criteria for inclusion in special education programs. This is merely a proposal for experimentation, and the field is currently reacting to it. Therefore, we must be content with out current policies and continue to strive for better ones.

For many resource room teachers this debate will have little or no impact. They are charged with providing appropriate services to each student. Whether or not the students are all classified the same or are in a cross-categorical classroom should not alter teaching practices. However, most practitioners recognize that when students are placed and grouped by a number of variables rather than by merely one classification, their job is easier because the students' needs are not as diverse. The needs of the students, not the administrative model employed, must dictate the program.

THE ROLE OF THE RESOURCE ROOM TEACHER

There is widespread agreement in the professional literature regarding the role of the special education resource room teacher. Wiederholt, Hammill, and Brown (1983) divide the responsibilities of the job into three major categories: (1) assessment, (2) teaching, and (3) consulting. Others have employed a wide variety of administrative structures to discuss similar role functions. For example, Jenkins and Mayhall (1976) differentiate between indirect and direct services. The former focuses on the identification of the academic and behavioral skills that must be taught, development and monitoring of the intervention plan, and ongoing communication with the regular classroom teacher. The latter are those services provided to the student. Reger (1973), one of the earliest proponents of the resource room model, believes that special education resource room teachers must provide regular classroom teachers with appropriate models for teaching the student with special needs. They carry out this function through consultation, as well as by more formal in-service training. The current thrust for more thorough staff development programs provides the resource room teacher with ample opportunity for engaging in this endeavor. As others have noted (Cienion, 1968; Hallerick, 1969; Sabatino, 1972), these functions are in addition to the assessment and teaching responsibilities.

To be sure, the role of the special education resource room teacher is more complex than is often realized. Reger (1972) has elevated the role to that of an "expert" and notes that in order to be an effective practitioner one must be cognizant of the major functions included within this role. Clearly these functions may vary from school district to district; however, it is evident that the evaluation of the educational problem, the development and implementation of the intervention plan, and the ongoing communication with regular educators will be major components of the role regardless of the particular setting in which the teacher is employed. Recently, an investigation was undertaken (Reiter, 1986) to examine the resource room teachers' perception of their role. Reiter's findings were consistent with those of other investigators in that the role was multifaceted. The remainder of this section will provide an overview of these three components of the special education resource room teacher's role.

The Educational Evaluation

Resource room teachers are typically responsible for evaluating the academic and behavioral skills of students who are enrolled in the resource room or who may be placed there in the future. Hammill and Bartel (1971) note that schools evaluate students for three reasons: classification, placement, and to enable them to plan an educational program. It is this last reason that is of critical importance to the resource room teacher. By definition, children attending the resource room spend most of their school day in a regular classroom. Therefore, the assessment should be related to the curriculum areas, whether they are the basic skills on the elementary level or the content areas on the middle and secondary levels (Deno and Merkin, 1977). Frequently, a disproportional amount of time is engaged in "diagnoses for identification versus diagnoses for teaching" (Hallahan and Kauffman, 1976). The former is characterized as formal, standardized testing, usually administered by a professional other than the teacher and done so outside the classroom setting. This testing typically satisfies the administrative charges of the school district but often fails to provide the teacher with adequate information upon which an educational program can be developed. Diagnosis for teaching accomplishes this goal. It is most likely criterion-referenced testing administered by the teacher in a low-structure, natural setting of the classroom and is directly related to the development of an intervention plan.

If resource room teachers are to develop intervention plans that are based on sound psychoeducational principles, then it is imperative that the selection of assessment tools is a thoughtful process that considers the particular educational setting of the student. In addition to being guided by general considerations regarding assessment (see Salvia and Ysseldyke, 1983), resource room teachers need to be aware of the curriculum validity of the procedures employed: that is, are they sensible and reasonable for the specific class and school in which the child is enrolled? Typically, this process relies heavily on criterion-referenced tests and behavioral assessment techniques. Chapter 2 will provide the reader with the skills necessary for engaging in effective assessment practices int he special education resource room.

The Intervention Plan

Typically, the highest percentage of a resource room teacher's time is spent on direct instruction with students. The number of specific methods and materials used in special education settings continues to grow at a rapid pace. The resource room teacher must keep abreast of these new techniques and materials and must be skilled in evaluating their effectiveness (see chapter 2). More importantly, the resource room teacher must have an underlying theory of instruction. This is not a new notion — Bruner (1966) discussed this idea nearly twenty years ago — but the message is perhaps more important today, especially for those involved in the education of students with special educational needs. Resource room teachers are constantly involved in making decisions regarding the needs of their students. Do students benefit from "tutoring" sessions in the resource room? Should one prepare them for the test on Friday? Does one remediate their basic skills? Does one employ an approach that provides the students with strategies that will enable them to learn more effectively? The teacher must be prepared to make these decisions on the basis of a conceptional framework of the purpose of a resource room. Without such a framework, decisions will be made based upon the momentary need with little thought to the overall operation of the program.

Generally speaking, the approach advocated here is the development of an intervention plan that remediates the students' weaknesses by focusing on their strengths (Johnson and Myklebust, 1967). The methodology employed should be similar to that used in the regular classroom (Deno and Merkin, 1977). The goals of instruction should be identical to those of the students' regular classroom counterparts.

The difference will be how these goals can be reached. A detailed discussion of academic programming will be presented in chapter 3.

Communicating with Regular Classroom Teachers

This final responsibility of the special education resource room teacher, consulting with teachers, is one of relative neglect. To be sure, there are resource room teachers who have the time and competence to carry out this function, but it is typically of low priority. Although there is agreement on the importance of communicating with regular educators, it is often an area fraught with difficulty. Cohen and Safran (1981) report that first-year resource room teachers rated working cooperatively with regular educators among their most significant problems. Furthermore, their regular classroom colleagues are often dissatisfied with their performance in this area (McLoughlin and Remer, 1983).

Given the reality that students who are placed in the resource room spend the majority of the school day with regular educators, it behooves those responsible for the "special education" to establish a cooperative, working relationship with those teachers. If the academic and behavioral skills taught in the resource room are to transfer to the regular classroom setting, the regular education must have a meaningful role in the process. This notion of teacher consultation is viewed as the key to a successful resource room program (McNamara, 1985).

Initially, special education resource room teachers must identify the needs of the staff in their particular building. This can be accomplished through the use of a simple questionnaire. McNamara (1981) reports that the following areas should be addressed:

1. The nature of the disorder of the student
2. Realistic goals for the youngsters while they are in the regular classroom
3. Methods and materials appropriate for instruction
4. Ways to evaluate the students' progress in the mainstream
5. How to communicate with parents of the mainstreamed students
6. Effective scheduling that does not interfere with normal classroom activities
7. The Individualized Education Program (IEP) of the student
8. The role and responsibilities of the special educator

Concurrently, the teacher should develop a brochure to be presented to the staff members during the first week of school. This will allow them to become familiar with the objectives of the resource room.

Ongoing academic and behavioral reporting systems are helpful; however, regularly scheduled face-to-face consultation will greatly enhance the cooperative nature of the relationship. Reger (1973) notes that the mere simplicity of this concept is at the root of its failure. To suggest, as Reger does, that 15 percent of teacher time should be spent in this activity is easily said; however, the reality is that it is not often accomplished. Deno and Merkin (1977) report on a program in which special education resource room teachers were provided with time to engage in consultation activities (25 percent of their school day). Within one month they reverted to 100 percent direct service to students, with no contact with regular education. The reason given was that it was more reinforcing working with their students. Although this may be true for many resource room teachers, they must become aware that it is not a viable option. Contacts with regular classroom teachers must be approached with the same rigor as contacts with students. Resource room teachers should take the opportunitites that will probably come about from the change to restrictive special and regular education (Will, 1986; Reynolds, Wang, and Walberg, 1987). The delivery of more effective programs for all children will need a strong partnership between special and regular educators. Chapter 3 provides a number of activities that will allow resource room teachers to select those strategies that are most applicable in their setting.

The Resource Room Teacher as a Member of an Interdisciplinary Team

In addition to juggling his or her responsibilities in the three roles noted above, the resource room teacher must become a member of the team, and as such must be able to contribute to this team. There are a number of professionals who may be members of this interdisciplinary team: the school psychologist, the school social worker, the speech and language pathologist, the occupational therapist, the physical therapist, the principal, the district administrator, the school nurse or physician, and a host of specialists such as a neurologist, psychiatrist, or physiatrist. Depending upon the school district and the needs of the student, any number of professionals may be included on this team. The effective resource room teacher will become aware of the role and responsibilities of each member of the team so that he or she will be able to provide useful information and reduce the possibility of duplicating information. It is not sufficient to have textbook information of these professionals because the way in which each school district, perhaps even each building, operationalizes each role may differ. For example, in many school districts school psychologists assess the intellectual, social, and emotional status of students as well as provide counseling services. However, in one particular district, a school social worker might provide the latter service. By becoming aware of this arrangement, the resource room teacher will be better able to identify key personnel when necessary. Awareness also prevents duplication; for example, he or she might be assessing the gross motor functioning of a student when this task has already been done by the physical therapist. Knowing how his or her team functions will enable the teacher to carry out responsibilities in an efficient and effective manner.

Role of the Resource Program Teacher: An Example

The following is an example of how one educational agency clarified the functions of the resource room teacher. The source is Suffolk County, N.Y., BOCES 2, The Resource Program Standards Committee (1986).

The role of the resource teacher is to support the classroom program by strengthening student basic skills, comprehension, or understanding of information so that the students can function successfully. Resource services may and should vary according to the unique profile of the student(s) being serviced.

Following are definitions of two widely used approaches that are common to many resource programs.

Basic Skills Instruction. The intent of this approach is to follow the appropriate learning sequence to improve the deficit area so that the student may acquire the basic academic skills necessary for academic progress. The emphasis is, therefore, deficit identification and instruction.

Learning Strategies Approach. This approach provides academic support for the regular classwork. Emphasis is placed on the attainment of ability with coursework and not on the area of deficit that is preventing the student from achieving success in the content area.

Application. A relation between these two models seems to have developed into a continuum from elementary to secondary levels.

On an elementary level, grades 1-3, the basic skills approach can offer the support a child needs to prepare and achieve success in academic areas.

Beginning in grade 4, a child who demonstrates below-level functioning in the basic areas (reading, math, handwriting, spelling) may need a developmental approach in conjunction with compensatory help in subject area information and comprehension.

Beyond junior high school, the shift becomes more toward the compensation of deficits and becomes better defined by other approaches that stress the attainment of abilities as they apply to specific coursework.

Recommendations.

1. The "Basic Skills Instruction Approach" should be used for early elementary grades when possible.
2. The "Learning Strategies Approach" should be used on the intermediate and secondary levels, with the use of subject area material (i.e., social studies, vocabulary to teach spelling and dictionary skills) when remedial intervention is necessary.
3. On the intermediate and secondary levels, the idea of functionality of learning should be taken into consideration. Awareness and incorporation of social, personal, and vocational skills should be addressed if students are to successfully function within the mainstream.

The conclusion of recent research is that there is no one correct model. Each student's needs require individual attention and diagnosis, necessarily yielding a unique approach to be taken.

Additional Roles. Based on the philosophy and goals of the Resource Program, a sufficient amount of time should be built into the resource teacher's schedule to allow efficient and thorough execution of the following duties:

1. Testing Responsibilities — Once a child has been shown to be academically delayed through application of achievement tests, the resource teacher should administer diagnostic tests to determine the proper approach to intervention.

   Specific domain testing, i.e., speech, hearing, IQ, should be administered by the appropriate personnel and made available for use by the resource teacher.

   Due to the nature of the Resource Program as temporary and supportive, the resource teacher should continue to administer formal and informal evaluations for the purpose of modification of intervention techniques and preparation for the eventual return to the mainstream.
2. Consultation Responsibilities — Resource teachers should maintain an ongoing consultative dialogue with the regular education staff

to provide feedback to classroom teachers on student progress and learning styles. Fifteen to 20 percent of their time should be devoted to this activity.

3. Resource Responsibilities — The resource room teacher should act as a resource person to the regular education staff in areas of support for the regular education students.
4. Transitional Responsibilities — The resource room teacher can provide support to a regular or special education teacher to aid in the provision of appropriate services (as specified in the pupil's individualized education program) when that pupil is transferring to a regular program or a program in a less restrictive environment.
5. COH Responsibilities — The resource teacher who administers the evaluation tests for a student should be invited to take part in the meeting at which recommendations are made to the COH. Resource teachers should take part in the periodic COH meetings for their students.
6. Other Responsibilities — Resource teachers should participate in multidisciplinary teams or any other building-level committees that involve the evaluation and progress of their students.

Resource teachers should maintain parent contact and have access to a social worker or other designated person to facilitate this contact when necessary.

2

The Development of the Resource Room

THE PHYSICAL SETTING

It is important to recognize that the physical setting of the resource room can have an impact on student behavior — both academic and social. The size, location, and appearance of the room are important considerations that should not be overlooked or minimized in the development of the resource room program. The manner in which each of these aspects is considered may either interfere with or facilitate student performance.

Size

There are innumerable tales of woe regarding the lack of sufficient space for resource room classes. Some teachers have to share their rooms with other specialists (reading, speech, etc.), others work in quarters that are clearly too small for students and equipment, and still others have no permanent room of their own, moving about the building with a cart full of supplies. The rationale for such practices appears to be that a relatively small number of students attend the resource room at any one time, and that therefore this setting can be much smaller than a typical classroom. In some school districts this picture is changing because of declining enrollment; with fewer students in the regular grades there are more classrooms available to be used as resource rooms.

The optimal size of a resource room should be that of a typical, regular education classroom. Perhaps there are situations in which the room could be smaller. However, when one considers what equipment is needed, it is difficult to justify a reduction in size. At the very least there has to be adequate space to enable the teacher to conduct small group lessons and individual lessons, provide for "quiet space" for students, store materials and student data, and have access to electrical outlets for audiovisual equipment. When the room is too small, students will often interfere with each other, especially those who have difficulty attending to tasks. It is unreasonable to ask a student who has an attentional deficit to remain on task in the face of so many blatant distractions. This is not to suggest that a stimulus-free environment is warranted, rather that there may well be too much going on in close physical proximity for this student to remain on task. Adequate space affords the student the opportunity to at least be available for learning. The manner in which the teacher uses that space will be considered below in the section on floor plans.

Location

A few years ago a local high school was observed to have a resource room program in a prefabricated module outside the school. Students attending this resource room program had to leave the main building and walk a short distance to receive special education services. This isolated setting kept the program from being integrated with the rest of the high school population. Students attending the resource room may have felt stigmatized, nondisabled students were ignorant of the program, and the teacher was cut off from her regular education colleagues. This is an extreme example of the implications of class location. However, it is still not unusual to have all resource rooms located in isolated, underutilized, or inapprorpriate sections of a school building.

When deciding on the location of the resource room, one must consider the grade placement of the students to be served and the organization of the building. On the elementary level, primary-grade students may be located in a particular wing or on a particular floor. The most logical location for the resource room would be in that wing or on that floor. If the resource room serves both primary- and intermediate-level students, then a location central to these two groups would be the most sensible. On the junior and high school level there may be more than one resource room. Once again, the location should be in close proximity to the students being served. This closeness reduces the travel time from the regular to the special education setting and, most importantly, increases opportunities for interaction between regular and special education personnel. One high school resource room teacher asked to have her room located next to the teacher's lounge, thereby enabling her to converse and consult with a large number of regular classroom teachers. The resource room program must be perceived as an integral part of the school. The proper location will help to reinforce this notion.

Appearance

The resource room should have a bright, cheerful, well-organized appearance. Students should get the message that the teacher cares enough about what goes on within the classroom to keep it attractive. And although it is clear that some schools have the financial resources to provide students with exceptional physical plants, few would deny that it takes very little to keep a classroom well maintained — even in a school building that is in disrepair. Care should be taken to make it an attractice environment, conducive to learning. Some teachers allow students to "decorate" the room; others have done so themselves. In either case, some effort should be taken to demonstrate to students that this is a special place.

Unfortunately, there are still some resource room teachers who cling to past theories that suggest that a classroom should be free from distraction and that attention can be harnessed by providing such a stimulus-free environment (Strauss and Kephart, 1955). This type of classroom is still in evidence in some resource room settings. The belief that attention can be increased in such an environment has never been empirically verified (Smith, 1983), yet vestiges of the theory remain. Resource room teachers must consider the needs of their students and, if appropriate, provide for a space that is free of most distractions. However, to set up a classroom so that virtually all stimulation is eliminated is unrealistic and, more importantly, will provide little opportunity to transfer skills developed in the resource room to the highly stimulating regular classroom setting.

Floor Plan

As mentioned above, each resource room should be able to accommodate enough desks, tables, and chairs for individual and small group instruction, audiovisual equipment, and a section for "quiet space." The floor plan in figure 1 illustrates that there is ample physical space to allow the students to move about the room without bumping into each other or interfering with the work of others. As the students enter the room, they proceed directly to their folders (see figure 2) and start on their daily assignments. The folders will also signal where they should go in the room: 0 = group work; □ = individual desk; ▭ = AV table, and so forth. Students who need or perfer a less distracting environment can go to the carrels.

The use of bookcases, file cabinets, and the like can serve as dividers and further enhance movement about the room in an orderly fashion. There are endless modifications on this plan. However, the physical arrangement of the room should always reflect the needs of the students, not the teacher's preference for a particular type of arrangement.

SCHEDULING

Special education resource room teachers frequently feel pulled in many directions. Nowhere is this more evident than in the task of scheduling. Schedules must be developed so that they conform to the administrative structure of the building, meet the needs of the students, do not interfere with the activities of the regular classroom, and allow the resource room teacher to comply with state regulations regarding student-teacher ratios. Clearly, this is not a simple task. It is important to have the involvement of the building principal in this procedure. Resource room teachers must have adequate time to consult with their regular education colleagues. Some schools have instituted a common period, or "x" period, prior to the start of the school day that allows for this type of communication. Too often, however, teachers are left to find time themselves. This problem only reinforces the notion that ongoing communication is not a valued practice in the school.

Once the schedule is established so that regular and special education teachers can communicate with one another, individual students must be scheduled into the resource room program. On the elementary level it is of critical importance to do this scheduling, in cooperation with the regular classroom teacher. The resource room teacher should set

Figure 1
Sample Floor Plan for a Resource Room

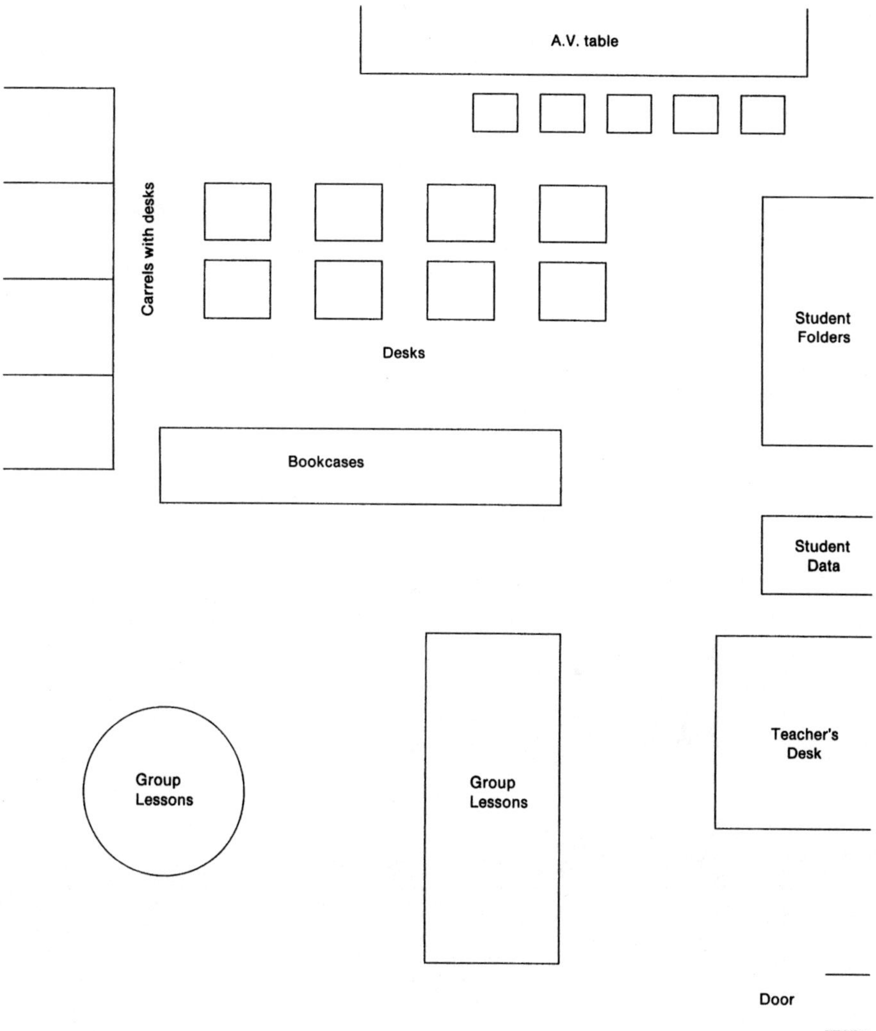

Figure 2
A Typical Student Folder

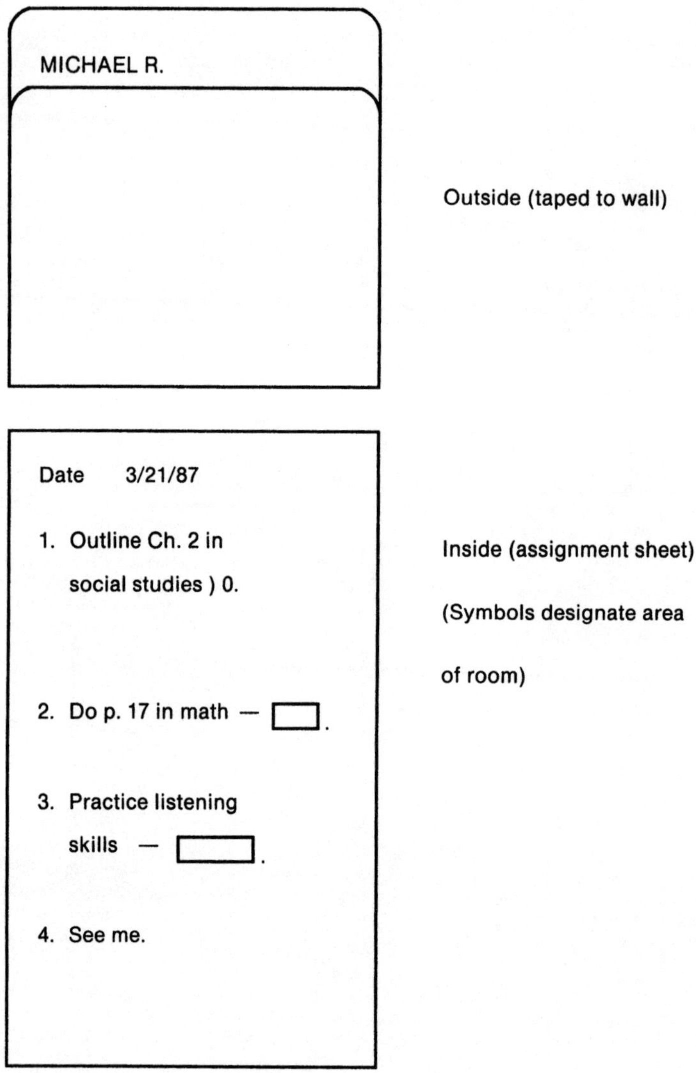

up a meeting in which both teachers can decide what would be the most reasonable period of time for the student to come to the resource room. Both teachers need to consider the strengths and weaknesses of the student, what he or she would be missing in the regular classroom during a difficult transition period, how the student feels about this part of the day, and so forth. Obviously, there will be times when compromises must be made. However, if the schedules are renegotiated every marking period, these decisions appear to be easier to accept by all concerned parties.

On the secondary level there is much more flexibility, and the resource room teacher must consult with guidance personnel to assist in the scheduling. Frequently students on this level attend the resource room during an elective period. Sometimes parents opt to eliminate certain subjects, such as a foreign language, and students then attend the resource room during that period. Parents and teachers need to consider if a student would need a particular course for a graduation requirement, postsecondary plans, or employment. There are no easy answers regarding the complexity of scheduling. However, when flexibility and reason prevail, most problems can be worked out.

All these considerations point to the fact that there is no "typical day" for a resource room teacher. To provide sample schedules and responsibilities may be misleading because the variation is so wide. In a survey of over twenty schedules and responsibilities conducted by the author, all of the teachers interviewed had a lopsided assignment of students; that is, they may have had one student during period 1, two during period 2, and five for the next two periods. Scheduling students for the resource room is obviously not a simple task.

In this same survey, all teachers had at least one period to consult with their regular education colleagues, and a few had two periods per day. One problem was that the period they had available was not always the period the regular classroom teacher had available. Therefore, a great deal of consultation occurred before and after school, during lunch, or haphazardly throughout the day. One school had a period prior to the beginning of the school day for this purpose, and it was extremely effective.

All teachers noted that they had frequent "walk-ins": students who came by to "take a test" or "needed a pass" or "needed help" in a wide variety of subjects. It was also not unusual to have a classroom teacher stop by during a class period with a specific concern regarding a resource room teacher. What clearly emerges from an examination of these schedules is that the typical day is very atypical and that this is no job for an inflexible individual.

SELECTION OF ASSESSMENT PROCEDURES

There are two general functions of assessment as it relates to special education students: (1) the determination of the disability for placement or eligibility purposes and (2) the collection of information necessary to plan effective programs (Tucker, 1985). Hallahan and Kauffman (1976) refer to the former as "diagnosis for identification" and to the latter as "diagnosis for teaching." Frequently, the resource room teacher is involved in both functions. Many school districts use the resource room teacher as a member of the multidisciplinary team that conducts formal evaluations. This task typically involves the administration and interpretation of standardized, norm-referenced formal tests. In addition, all resource room teachers must develop data collection procedures to enable them to plan effective programs for their students and to monitor the students' progress in such programs. This section will discuss both aspects of assessment.

Purpose of Assessment

Salvia and Ysseldyke (1985) note that the only legitimate purpose of psychoeducational assessment is the collection of educationally relevant information. Too often this purpose is forgotten and clinicians engage in a "shot-gun" approach to assessment, whereby a significant amount of useless information is generated. The resource room teacher who is responsible for educational evaluations must be aware of the purpose of the assessment, as well as the technical aspects of a particular device being employed. It may well be that a battery of tests is given to all referrals to special education. However, in most cases the evaluator can choose the particular assessment tool. Resource room teachers need to approach this task with a great deal of thought because the information generated in any evaluation is related to the devices employed. An unreliable, nonvalid device will provide unreliable, nonvalid information.

There are a number of useful resources available for this purpose. *Tests in Print* and *Mental Measurement Yearbooks* are available in most college and university libraries and provide readers with up-to-date information on a large number of assessment tools. If the resource room teacher does not have access to them through a library, they can be obtained from the Buros Institute of Mental Measurement, 135 Bancroft Hall, University of Nebraska, Lincoln, Nebraska 68588-0348. A perusal of current journals, such as the *Journal of Learning Disabilities, Journal of Special Education, Journal of Behavioral Assessment, Journal of Remedial and Special Education,* and *Exceptional Children*, to name a few, will frequently have reports or reviews on a particular assessment instrument. Current textbooks on assessment, such as that by Salvia and Ysseldyke (1985), will also help keep educational evaluations abreast of tests that are reliable, valid, and technically sound and that will provide the information that teachers desire.

The resource room teacher may also want to refer to the table developed by Taylor (1984) that lists frequently used assessment devices, their suggested use, the target population, any special considerations, and the relevance for exceptional students (see table 1).

Obviously, it is imperative that the resource room teacher responsible for formal assessment procedures is competent in this area. The information listed in table 1 is to be used as a resource by those who are competent diagnosticians. Those who are in need of additional basic information should consult Taylor (1984) and Salvia and Upseldyke (1985) or receive additional training.

It is important that all resource room teachers are aware that 'there is little evidence that any assessment intended to diagnose the handicap of a student provides data relevant to the educational instruction needed by that student" (Tucker, 1985, p. 201). Therefore, the practice of evaluating students solely with formal, standardized tests cannot be justified. Only when these instruments are employed in conjunction with procedures that enable the clinician to gather educationally relevant information can they benefit the student. The following section will discuss these informal, data-gathering procedures.

Diagnosis for Teaching

Resource room teachers must be able to assess skills in the regular and special education setting in a wide variety of curriculum areas. The information generated for these assessments must be useful in the development of an effective plan of instruction that can be implemented in the resource room or the regular classroom setting. These procedures must not take such an inordinate amount of time that the resource room teacher is always testing and rarely teaching. Zigmond, Vallecorsa, and Silverman (1983) have developed the following twelve-step strategy that can serve as a framework for this data collection procedure:

1. Decide what to assess.
2. Select or develop a skill hierarchy.
3. Decide where to begin.
4. Select or develop a survey instrument.
5. Get ready to test.

Table 1
Frequently Used Assessment Instruments

Instrument or Technique	Suggested Use: Prereferral		Suggested Use: Postreferral					Target Population						Special Considerations	Educational Reference for Exceptional Students
	Screening and initial Identification	Informal Determination and Evaluation of Teaching Programs and Strategies	Determination of Current Performance Level and Educational Need	Decisions about Classification and Program Placement	IEP Goals	IEP Objectives	IEP Evaluation	Mild/Moderate	Severe/Profound	Preschool	Elementary Age	Secondary Age	Adult		
Denver Developmental Screening Test	X							X	X	X				Limited technical aspects, particularly validity and standardization	limited
Meeting Street School Screening Test	X							X		X	X			Heavily weighted toward perceptual motor ability	limited
Northwestern Syntax Screening Test	X							X		X	X			Extremely limited technical aspects; should be used for rough screening	limited
Slingerland Tests	X	X						X		X	X			No technical data available; should be used informally; tedious scoring	adequate
Boehm Test of Basic Concepts	X	X			X			X		X	X			Best used informally; normative information is not that important	useful
First Grade Screening Test	X							X		X	X			Heavily weighted toward vocabulary; has an overly rigid scoring system	limited
Metropolitan Readiness Test	X							X		X	X			Good technical aspects; is very comprehensive	useful

Instrument or Technique	Screening and initial Identification	Informal Determination and Evaluation of Teaching Programs and Strategies	Determination of Current Performance Level and Educational Need	Decisions about Classification and Program Placement	IEP Goals	IEP Objectives	IEP Evaluation	Mild/Moderate	Severe/Profound	Preschool	Elementary Age	Secondary Age	Adult	Special Considerations	Educational Reference for Exceptional Students
	Prereferral		*Postreferral*												
	Suggested Use							*Target Population*							
California Achievement Tests	X							X			X	X		Adequate technical aspects; criterion referenced objectives are available	adequate
Iowa Test of Basic Skills	X							X			X	X		Adequate technical aspects; standardized concurrently with a group intelligence test (Cognitive Abilities Test)	adequate
Metropolitan Achievement Tests	X	X						X			X	X		Good technical aspects; provides specific objectives as well as overall scores	useful
SRA Achievement Series	X							X			X	X		Adequate technical aspects; standardized with a group intelligence test (Educational Ability Series)	adequate
Stanford Achievement Tests	X	X						X			X	X		Good technical aspects; one of the more popular group achievement tests	useful
Tests of Achievement and Proficiency	X							X			X	X		Upward extension of the Iowa Test of Basic Skills	adequate
Peabody Individual Achievement Test	X	X	X		X			X			X	X		Adequate technical aspects; does not require written responses; equivocal research with exceptional students	adequate
Wide Range Achievement Test	X	X	X		X			X		X	X	X	X	Limited technical aspects; results often overused; no reading comprehension measure	adequate

Instrument or Technique	Suggested Use — Prereferral: Screening and initial Identification	Suggested Use — Prereferral: Informal Determination and Evaluation of Teaching Programs and Strategies	Suggested Use — Postreferral: Determination of Current Performance Level and Educational Need	Suggested Use — Postreferral: Decisions about Classification and Program Placement	Suggested Use — Postreferral: IEP Goals	Suggested Use — Postreferral: IEP Objectives	Suggested Use — Postreferral: IEP Evaluation	Target Population: Mild/Moderate	Target Population: Severe/Profound	Target Population: Preschool	Target Population: Elementary Age	Target Population: Secondary Age	Target Population: Adult	Special Considerations	Educational Reference for Exceptional Students
Gray Oral Reading Test	X	X						X			X	X		Very limited technical aspects, error analysis should be used	limited
Gilmore Oral Reading Test	X							X			X			Very limited technical aspects, error analysis should be used	limited
Durrell Analysis of Reading Difficulty		X	X		X			X			X			Normative data are of little value, should be used informally	adequate
Diagnostic Reading Scales		X	X		X			X			X			Reading levels determined should be used as guidelines only, error analysis could be useful	adequate
Stanford Diagnostic Reading Test	X		X		X			X			X	X		Well constructed; can be group-administered, does not yield specific instructional information	useful
Test of Reading Comprehension	X							X			X	X		Heavily weighted toward vocabulary and syntex	limited
Woodcock Reading Mastery Scales	X		X		X			X			X			Widely used test, has unusual format; equivocal research with exceptional students	limited
Key Math Diagnostic Arithmetic Test	X	X	X		X			X			X	X		Very popular test; technical aspects are limited and its normative use should be downplayed	adequate
Stanford Diagnostic Mathematics Test	X		X		X			X			X	X		Good technical aspects, can be group-administered	useful
Test of Written Spelling	X	X	X		X			X			X			One of the few tests that yields normative information in spelling, best used informally, however	useful

Instrument or Technique	Screening and initial Identification	Informal Determination and Evaluation of Teaching Programs and Strategies	Determination of Current Performance Level and Educational Need	Decisions about Classification and Program Placement	IEP Goals	IEP Objectives	IEP Evaluation	Mild/Moderate	Severe/Profound	Preschool	Elementary Age	Secondary Age	Adult		Educational Reference for Exceptional Students
	Prereferral		*Postreferral*												
	Suggested Use							*Target Population*						*Special Considerations*	
Group Administered Intelligence Tests	X							X		X	X	X	X	Use for screening only, resemble group achievement tests in format and, to a certain extent, content	limited
Wechsler Intelligence Scale for Children Revised			X	X				X			X	X		Very widely used; well constructed; profile analyses of subtests should be avoided	useful
Goodenough Harris Drawing Test	X							X		X	X			Very limited technical aspects; should not be used as a sole measure of intelligence	very limited
Kaufman Assessment Battery for Children			X	X	X			X		X	X			Well constructed, measures both acquired knowledge and intelligence; includes norms for different sociocultural groups	useful
McCarthy Scales of Children's Abilities			X	X				X			X	X		Well constructed; measures areas that are important to early school success	useful
Slosson Intelligence Test	X							X		X	X	X	X	Use for screening only; uses a ratio IQ format; easy to administer	limited
Woodcock-Johnson Psychoeducational Battery			X	X	X			X		X	X	X	X	Measures both aptitude and achievement; "cluster" scores should not be overinterpreted	adequate

Instrument or Technique	Screening and initial Identification	Informal Determination and Evaluation of Teaching Programs and Strategies	Determination of Current Performance Level and Educational Need	Decisions about Classification and Program Placement	IEP Goals	IEP Objectives	IEP Evaluation	Mild/Moderate	Severe/Profound	Preschool	Elementary Age	Secondary Age	Adult	Special Considerations	Educational Reference for Exceptional Students
	Prereferral		*Postreferral*												
	Suggested Use							*Target Population*						*Special Considerations*	
Adaptive Behavior Inventory for Children				X				X			X			Part of the System of Multicultural Pluralistic Assessment; used primarily to help "declassify" minority children	adequate
AAMD Adaptive Behavior Scale			X	X	X			X	X	X	X	X	X	Technical aspects of Part Two have been questioned, has limited use for most severely retarded individuals	adequate
AAMD Adaptive Behavior Scale-SE			X	X	X			X		X	X	X		Potentially useful instrument to aid in classification and placement decisions	useful
Balthazar Scales of Adaptive Behavior			X		X	X			X		X	X	X	Best to use informally; the normative aspect is extremely limited	limited
Cain-Levine Social Competency Scale	X		X		X			X			X			Does not yield specific information for programming, validity data are lacking	limited
Camelot Behavioral Checklist	X		X		X			X			X	X	X	Does not yield specific information for programming, limited technical aspects	limited
Comprehensive Test of Adaptive Behavior			X	X	X	X		X	X	X	X	X		Potentially useful instrument for the overall measurement of adaptive behavior	useful
TARC Assessment System	X		X		X				X	X	X	X		Limited technical aspects; specific information is not yielded	limited
Preschool Attainment Record			X		X			X	X	X				Use informally to determine strengths and weaknesses	limited
Vineland Adaptive Behavior Scales			X	X	X	X		X	X	X	X	X		Potentially useful instrument for the overall measurement of adaptive behavior	very useful

Instrument or Technique	Screening and initial Identification	Informal Determination and Evaluation of Teaching Programs and Strategies	Determination of Current Performance Level and Educational Need	Decisions about Classification and Program Placement	IEP Goals	IEP Objectives	IEP Evaluation	Mild/Moderate	Severe/Profound	Preschool	Elementary Age	Secondary Age	Adult	*Special Considerations*	Educational Reference for Exceptional Students
	Prereferral		*Postreferral*												
	Suggested Use							*Target Population*							
Beniker Visual Motor Gestalt Test (Koppill)	X	X						X			X			Frequently used test that is often mis-used widely researched instrument	adequate
Developmental Test of Visual Motor Integration	X	X						X		X	X	X		Limited technical aspects; somewhat subjective scoring system	limited
Developmental Test of Visual Perception	X							X		X	X			Very limited technical aspects; has little practical use	very limited
Motor Free Visual Perception Test	X	X						X		X	X			Limited technical aspects; only test of visual perception without a motor component	limited
Auditory Discrimination Test	X	X						X		X	X			Limited technical aspects; use with children who speak nonstandard English is not recommended	limited
G F W Test of Auditory Discrimination	X	X						X		X	X	X	X	Limited technical aspects; noise subtest is particularly questionable	limited
Bruininks Oserelsky Test of Motor Proficiency	X	X	X					X			X			One of the few tests that measures both line and gross motor abilities	adequate
Purdue Perceptual Motor Survey	X							X			X			Very limited technical aspects; based on Kephart's theory of perceptual motor match	very limited

Instrument or Technique	Suggested Use							Target Population						Special Considerations	Educational Reference for Exceptional Students
	Prereferral		Postreferral												
	Screening and initial Identification	Informal Determination and Evaluation of Teaching Programs and Strategies	Determination of Current Performance Level and Educational Need	Decisions about Classification and Program Placement	IEP Goals	IEP Objectives	IEP Evaluation	Mild/Moderate	Severe/Profound	Preschool	Elementary Age	Secondary Age	Adult		
Behavior Problem Checklist	X		X		X			X			X			Adequate technical aspects; has some empirical support in the literature	useful
Behavior Rating Profile	X		X		X			X			X			Student is evaluated by a number of individuals in a number of settings; validity data are lacking	adequate
Burks Behavior Rating Scale	X		X		X			X			X			Limited technical aspects; results are subject to misinterpretation	limited
Devereux Elementary School Behavior Rating Scale	X		X		X			X			X			Somewhat limited technical aspects; relatively popular instrument	adequate
Walker Problem Behavior Checklist	X							X			X			Limited validity data; is a quick screening device	adequate
Projective Techniques				X				X			X	X	X	Losing popularity in special education; very little evidence of reliability or validity for most of these instruments	very limited
Self-Concept Scales	X							X			X	X	X	Most lack validity data; many use a self-report system to obtain the scores	limited
Inventories and Questionnaires				X				X			X	X	X	Most have limited technical aspects, most are designed for adolescents and adults	limited

Instrument or Technique	Screening and initial Identification	Informal Determination and Evaluation of Teaching Programs and Strategies	Determination of Current Performance Level and Educational Need	Decisions about Classification and Program Placement	IEP Goals	IEP Objectives	IEP Evaluation	Mild/Moderate	Severe/Profound	Preschool	Elementary Age	Secondary Age	Adult	Special Considerations	Educational Reference for Exceptional Students
	Prereferral		*Postreferral*												
	Suggested Use							*Target Population*							
Peabody Picture Vocabulary Test A	X							X		X	X	X	X	Can be used with individuals with speech and motor handicaps, results should not be overinterpreted	useful
Clinical Evaluation of Language Functions		X	X		X			X			X	X		Best used informally; limited validity data, measures language processing and production	adequate
Illinois Test of Psycholinguistic Abilities	X							X		X	X			Widely used and abused instrument; extremely limited technical aspects	very limited
Test of Language Development	X	X	X		X			X		X	X			Based on a sound theoretical model; validity data are lacking	adequate
Test of Adolescent Language	X	X	X		X			X				X		One of the few tests designed to measure language abilities of older students; validity data are lacking	adequate
Test of Written Language	X	X	X		X			X			X			Measures an important and often overlooked area; technical aspects are somewhat limited	adequate

Instrument or Technique	Screening and initial Identification	Informal Determination and Evaluation of Teaching Programs and Strategies	Determination of Current Performance Level and Educational Need	Decisions about Classification and Program Placement	IEP Goals	IEP Objectives	IEP Evaluation	Mild/Moderate	Severe/Profound	Preschool	Elementary Age	Secondary Age	Adult	Special Considerations	Educational Reference for Exceptional Students
	Prereferral		*Postreferral*												
	Suggested Use							*Target Population*							
Brigance Inventory of Basic Skills		x	x		x	x	x	x				x		Includes objectives for each item, used in IEP development (elementary)	useful
Brigance Inventory of Essential Skills		x	x		x	x	x	x				x		Includes objectives for each item used in IEP development (secondary)	useful
Brigance Comprehensive Inventory of Basic Skills		x	x		x	x	x	x			x	x		Similar to other Brigance Inventories in format, might be appropriate with students in the later elementary grades	useful
Criterion Test of Basic Skills	x	x	x		x			x			x			Information yielded is not very specific suggested teaching strategies are simplified	limited
Multilevel Academic Skill Inventory	x	x	x		x	x	x	x			x			Well constructed and comprehensive, use for screening and programming	very useful
Mastery An Evaluation Tool	x	x	x		x			x			x	x		Use for screening & monitoring progress rather than for educational programming	adequate
Diagnosis An Instructional Aid in Reading	x	x	x		x	x	x	x			x			Can be used for screening and educational programming test items are correlated with instructional materials	very useful
Informal Reading Inventories	x	x	x		x			x			x	x		Most measure word recognition and comprehension skills	useful
Diagnosis An Instructional Aid in Mathematics	x	x	x		x	x	x	x			x			Can be used for screening and programming test items are correlated with instructional materials	very useful
Enright Inventory of Arithmetic Skills	x	x	x		x	x	x	x			x			Used to determine specific math objectives error analysis is recommended	useful
Mathematics Concepts Inventory		x	x		x	x	x	x			x			Includes curriculum materials for each of the 240 items	adequate
Spellmaster	x	x	x		x			x			x			Information from error analysis is most valuable	adequate

Instrument or Technique	Screening and initial Identification	Informal Determination and Evaluation of Teaching Programs and Strategies	Determination of Current Performance Level and Educational Need	Decisions about Classification and Program Placement	IEP Goals	IEP Objectives	IEP Evaluation	Mild/Moderate	Severe/Profound	Preschool	Elementary Age	Secondary Age	Adult	*Special Considerations*	Educational Reference for Exceptional Students
	Prereferral		*Postreferral*												
	Suggested Use							*Target Population*							
Behavioral Characteristics Progression			X		X	X	X	X	X	X				Books of instructional suggestions that are correlated with each item as available	useful
Brigance Inventory of Early Development			X		X	X	X	X	X	X				Includes objectives for each item; developmental age equivalents should be used informally only	useful
Callier-Azusa			X		X				X	X				Designed for use with deaf-blind children, age equivalents should be used informally only	adequate
Learning Accomplishment Profile			X		X	X	X	X	X	X				Not particularly appropriate for more severely handicapped students; sequencing of some items is questionable	limited
Project MEMPHIS	X		X		X	X	X		X	X				Comprehensive package used for screening, programming & program monitoring	adequate
Pennsylvania Training Model	X		X		X	X	X		X	X				Comprehensive package used for screening, programming & program monitoring	useful
Uniform Performance Assessment System			X		X	X	X	X	X	X				Includes a code for any test adaptations that are necessary, age equivalents should be used informally only	adequate
Vulpe Assessment Battery			X		X	X	X	X	X	X				Has a tedious scoring system that does yield important programmatic information	useful

Note. All these instruments can be used with older, severely handicapped individuals, the majority of these instruments are appropropriate for those who have developmental ages up to six years

6. Administer the survey.
7. Note errors and performance style.
8. Analyze findings and summarize outcomes.
9. Hypothesize reasons for errors and determine areas to probe.
10. Probe.
11. Complete record-keeping forms and generate teaching objectives.
12. Start teaching; update assessment information.

These twelve steps can be even more useful to the resource room teacher if the principles of Curriculum Based Assessment (CBA) are employed. "In CBA the essential area of success in education is the student's progress in the curriculum of the local school" (Tucker, 1985, p. 199). A number of researchers (Anderson-Inman, 1986; Deshler and Schumacher, 1986; Palincsar, 1986) have suggested that the effectiveness of the resource room program should be judged by the student's performance in regular education settings. Therefore, it appears that a reasonable approach to assessment is to employ regular classroom materials as much as possible. It is of little consolation if a student performs well on a standardized measure and in the resource room yet is failing in his or her regular classroom. Therefore, throughout the following discussion of the twelve-step strategy, the frame of reference will be performance in the regular classroom.

Step 1 — **Decide what to assess.**

Students referred to the resource room will have an area or areas of deficiency noted on their individualized education program (IEP); therefore the area(s) to assess would appear in terms of a performance or a specific standardized test. For example, one might read, "Julie's major area of deficiency is in auditory processing" or "Mark appears to have difficulty with visual-motor-integration tasks." Alone, this type of information will not enable the teacher to develop an effective intervention plan. Therefore, the job of the resource room teacher is to decide how these deficiencies will manifest themselves in the regular classroom. This decision obviously necessitates a great deal of knowledge regarding exactly what goes on in each class of the students receiving resource room assistances. Initially, this task may appear to be overwhelming, yet there are strategies that can be effective (see chapter 4).

Step 2 — **Select or develop a skill hierarchy.**

Before selecting or developing a skill hierarchy, the resource room teacher must examine the text used in the regular class, any course outlines, and the teacher's methods of presentation. This will enable the teacher to employ a hierarchy that relates to the regular class curriculum and organization. Skills should be arranged in an orderly fashion from the easiest to the most difficult. At times, this arrangement will be arbitrary, yet one must use one's "best guess" as to where a skill belongs. Initially, this task is time-consuming, yet over the year the resource room teacher will have accumulated a great deal of information and so will not have to engage in the entire process each school year, just fill in areas in which there are gaps.

Step 3 — **Decide where to begin.**

In order to maximize one's efforts, one needs to pinpoint the range of skills that need to be assesed. Information can be obtained from previous tests, IEP's, and former and current teachers. This information will eliminate the need to administer an entire survey when only a grade or two would suffice. Moreover, overtesting can lead to fatigue on the part of the student and may negatively influence performance.

Step 4 — **Select or develop a survey instrument.**

What will the resource room teacher use to obtain the information necessary to plan a program? What is the purpose of the survey instrument? Once again, this instrument should approximate regular classroom instruction as much as possible. For example, if the student's area of deficiency is spelling (step 1) and he or she is currently in the ninth grade (step 2), then a reasonable spelling survey would be a list of words randomly selected from the various content areas. If the administration of an oral reading paragraph (step 1) is necessary, then it makes sense to employ the reading series that the student will use every day, not some commercially available informal reading inventory. The method of response should also be considered. If written responses are required in the regular classroom, it is important to assess this skill. Although it is important and useful diagnostic information to know that a student can select the correctly spelled word from a group of four, if he or she is never presented with this response in the regular classroom it will not help to develop an intervention plan to remediate his or her deficiency. This is not to suggest that this information is not useful to share with regular classroom teachers so that modification can be made. It simply suggests that the initial assessment should reflect regular classroom performance — those areas in which the students can succeed and those areas in which they may have difficulty. Modifications and adaptations can be explored when further areas of concern are probed (step 10).

Step 5 — **Get ready to test.**

In order to get the optional performance from students one must ensure that they are relaxed and comfortable. A low-structure, natural setting helps create a relaxed atmosphere. Any equipment that is to be used must be in proper working order, and the student must know how to operate it. The area in which the student will be assessed should be free from distraction and interruption, yet not sterile.

Step 6 — **Administrator the survey.**

Step 7 — **Note errors and performance style.**

Steps 6 and 7 can be viewed as one. The purpose of the survey is to observe what skills the students possess, what skills they do not possess, and how they approach tasks. Throughout the administration of the survey, the teacher should note all aspects of the students' performance for the purpose of replicating that performance at a later time. The teacher will want to be able to reconstruct the assessment to the maximum extent possible in order to analyze the students' performance. The manner in which students approach the task is as important as the number correct. Do they respond to reinforcement? Are they easily frustrated? How do they hold the pencil? Do they possess adequate oral language skills? Do they appear to understand direction? These and many other responses to tasks will be valuable diagnostic information when one begins to analyze student performance (step 8) and formulate hypotheses (step 9). Inexperienced teachers frequently feel that they miss much of this "clinical" information because they are concentrating on the actual administration of the survey. The more frequently one engages in the assessment process the more these skills will become more natural. "Practicing" these skills with colleagues will also help shore up this very important competency

Step 8 — **Analyze findings and summarize outcomes.**

Having completed the survey, the teacher must next examine it to determine if a pattern emerges. He or she may find, for example, that all tasks requiring sequencing pose a problem for the student or that any task requiring written expression is difficult. By carefully examining the specific findings, the teacher may be able to pinpoint the problem with more precision. One should also determine in what areas the student is competent. This knowledge is also helpful in identifying areas that are in need of additional practice. The teacher should summarize the information in any way that helps formulate hypotheses. A simple form (see figure 3) or a more sophisticated form, as described in the Zigmond et al. (1983) text, can be employed.

Figure 3
Summary Form for Analyzing Assessment Findings

Name:
Grade:
Regular classroom teacher(s):
Area surveyed:

	Strengths	Weaknesses

Hypotheses:

Areas to probe:

Step 9 — **Hypothesize reasons for errors and determine areas to probe.**

The resource room teacher must next try to determine why the student's performance is the way it is. He or she can hypothesize that it resulted from the way in which the information was presented to the student, the process in which the student was required to engage, or the output or response the student had to make. It is important to recognize that the reasons for performance may not be perfectly clear, but it is still necessary to formulate reasonable hypotheses in order to further explore the area(s) of concern.

Step 10 — **Probe.**

By manipulating the input modality, the learning process, and/or the output modality the teacher can gain additional insight on how the student performs on various tasks. This step adds refinement to the hypothesis and enables the teacher to develop an initial plan of instruction.

Step 11 — **Complete record-keeping forms and generate teaching objectives.**

One decides what to teach on the basis of what one knows. The teacher begins by formulating objectives in cooperation with the regular classroom teacher. These objectives should be observable and measurable and, in many cases, should form the foundation for report card grades. (More will be said about grades later.)

Step 12 — **Start teaching; update assessment information.**

Assessment is ongoing, dynamic process. Once the resource room teacher decides what to teach, he or she should set up an evaluation plan that enables him or her to decide whether or not the material has been learned. The data collection procedure can be as simple or as complex as one likes. All that is important is that progress is recorded at frequent intervals and that decisions as to what and how to teach are based on demonstrated performances. For example, one could record the number of pages completed in a textbook, the test scores in a science class, or the frequency of completion of homework (see figure 4).
More complex procedures can be found in Howell and Morehead (1987), where precision teaching and data-based program modification procedures are described. These may be beyond the needs of most resource room teachers, yet they should not be discounted for those teachers possessing the necessary behavorial background.

Figure 4
Sample Ways to Assess Progress

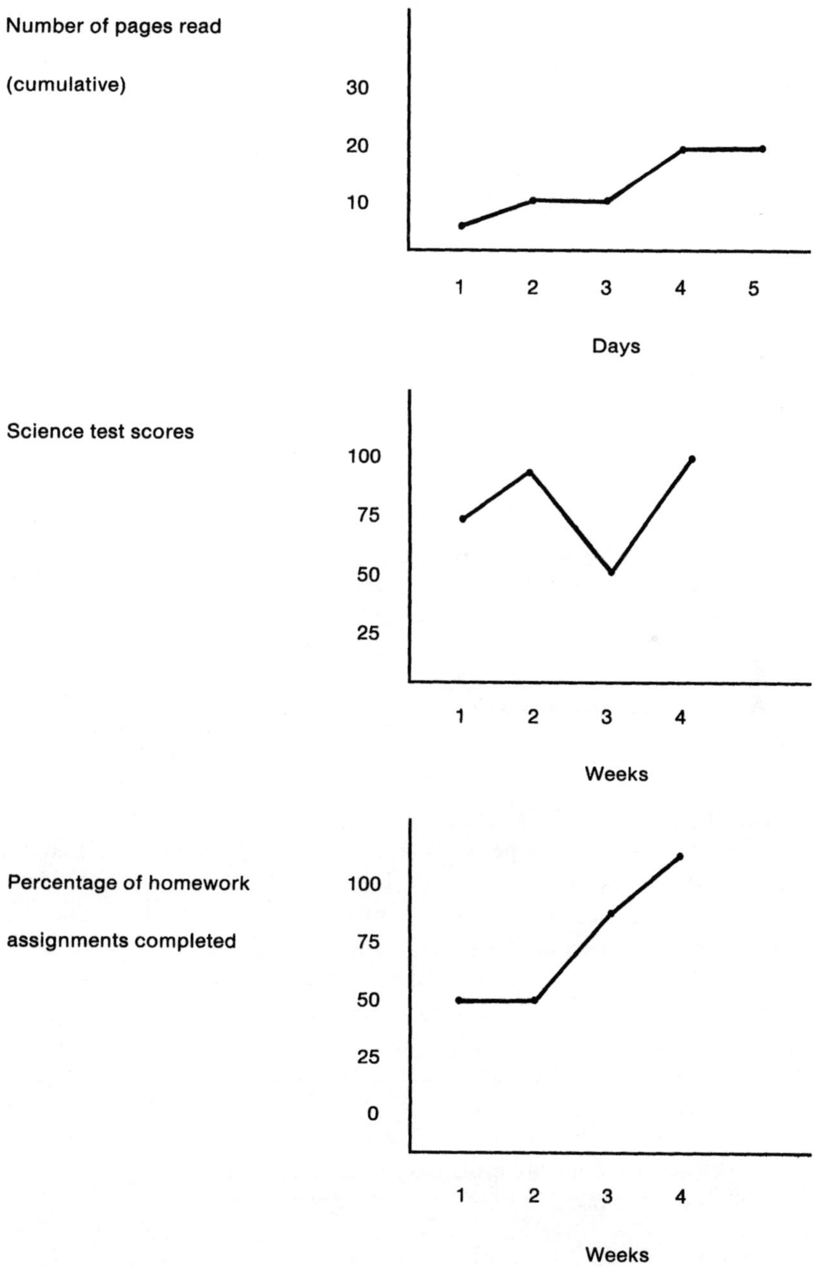

To be sure, the assessment process is fraught with problems. However, many of these can be minimized if resource room teachers treat all information gathered as inferential, NOT factual; if they formulate hypotheses regarding student performance, NOT statements that appear to be carved in stone; and if they teach in such a way that they can affirm or reject the hypotheses and continue the circular process of test-teach-test.

SELECTION OF INSTRUCTIONAL MATERIALS

The effective and efficient use of instructional materials is of critical importance for resource room teachers. In an educational setting where time on task is limited, teachers must be able to select materials that clearly meet the needs of the students, not merely pass the time. Unfortunately, this can be a difficult task for the novice resource room teacher. The availability of instructional materials appears to be increasing rapidly, and teachers frequently succumb to good packaging and promotion rather than the effectiveness of the product. The purpose of this section is to provide resource room teachers with the skills necessary to carefully analyze and select the instructional materials to be used in the resource room and, at times, in the regular education setting.

Analysis of Materials

Watson and Van Etten (1976) state that materials analysis should answer the following questions: "(1) What are the characteristics of the person for whom the material was designed? (2) What is the material like? That is, how is it organized? How is the information presented? What does the learner have to do with the materials? How does the learner get feedback on his performance? How is learner performance evaluated? (3) What is required of the teacher? (4) What data are available to indicate whether the program works or is worth the money?" (p. 13). In order to answer these questions, they developed a Materials Evaluation Form. The form (figure 5) is fairly simple to complete. Frequently, the resource room teacher will not be able to complete every response because the authors and publishers of the materials may not have provided sufficient information. In particular, one must be wary of materials that provide no data on their effectiveness.

Figure 5

Materials Evaluation Form (from Watson and Van Etten, 1976, pp. 15-17).

Title: ____________________

Author: ____________________

Publisher: ____________________

Address: ____________________

____

Cost: ____________

1. **LEARNER CHARACTERISTICS**

a. Chronological age:

b. Grade level:

c. Mental age:

d. Reading level:

e. Specific population for which material was designed:

f. Developmental age of concepts in instructions and activities:

g. Level of physical development required:

_____ Major factor _____ Minor factor _____Not important

Comment: ____________________

____

____

2. **MATERIAL PURPOSE**

a. What does material say it will do? ____________________

____

b. Objectives:

________ Behavioral ________ Nonbehavioral

3. **ORGANIZATION**

_______________ Lessons, explain

_______________ Units, explain

_______________ Chapters, explain

Other ____

4. **MATERIALS FORMAT**

________ Live verbal input

________ Records

________ Tapes

________ Film (bw/color)

________ Filmstrip (bw/color)

________ Posters (bw/color)

 ________ Consumable

 ________ Nonconsumable

________ Worksheets

________ Worksheets

 ________ Consumable

 ________ Nonconsumable

________ Textbook

________ Flashcards (bw/color)

________ Models

________ Demonstration

________ Programmed

5. **PRIMARY SENSORY PATH USED TO TRANSFER INFORMATION**

________ Auditory (lectures, tapes, records, etc.)

________ Audio-visual (tape and worksheets, sound film, etc.)

________ Visual (filmstrips, flashcards, worksheets, workbooks, texbooks, etc.)

________ Tactile-kinesthetic (raised surface, beaded, etc.)

________ Olfactory (scent bottles)

6. **SPACE REQUIREMENTS:** ____________________________

7. **TIME REQUIREMENTS:** ____________________________

8. **LEARNER INTERACTION**

_______ Motor

_______ Physical activity (dance, jump, etc.)

_______ Manipulation (beads, puzzles, etc.)

_______ Write a response

_______ Mark a response

_______ Other _______________________________

_______ Verbal

_______ Answers questions

_______ Repeats information

_______ Spontaneous contribution

_______ Other _______________________________

_______ Visual-Motor

_______ Copying tasks (bead or block patterns, etc.)

_______ Tracing

_______ Other _______________________________

_______ Visual

_______ Read

_______ Observe

_______ Matching

_______ Other _______________________________

9. **LEARNER KNOWLEDGE OF PROGRESS**

a. How do teacher and student know response is correct?

__________ Teacher checks student's work

__________ Self-checking by student when work is complete

__________ Immediate feedback process of some kind

Comment: ____

____

10. **EVALUATION AND DATA-RECORDING PROCEDURES**

a. How is starting point of instruction established?

_______ Written test ______ Performance test ________ Criterion test

_______ Checklist ______ Oral test ________ Direct and continuous measurement

_______ Direct and noncontinous measurement

_______ Other ____________________________________

Comment: ____

____

b. How is mastery of content demonstrated and recorded?

______ Written test ______ Performance test ________ Criterion test

______ Checklist ______ Oral test ________ Direct and continuous measurement

_______ Direct and noncontinous measurement

_______ Other ____________________________________

c. Data forms provided:

_______ Yes _______ No

d. Are criteria for acceptable performance stated?

_______ Yes, explain ____

_______ No, explain ____

Comment: ____

____

____

11. **TEACHER INVOLVEMENT REQUIRED: TEACHER PREPARATION**
(Check one)

_____ Extensive _____ Minimal _____ Reasonable

Teacher involvement during time in use:

_____ Constant interaction

_____ Teacher introduces and student completes

_____ Supportive help or monitor role

_____ Virtually none or none at all

Teacher responsibility when student is through with material:

_____ Teacher must check and provide feedback

_____ Virtually none or none at all

12. **TEACHER AIDS: IS THERE A TEACHER'S GUIDE OR MANUAL?**

___ Yes ___ No

If yes, what does it include?

______ Script

______ Annotated copy of student material

______ Background information

______ Extended activities

______ Follow-up activities

______ Other ____

Comment: ____

____

13. **POTPOURRI**

General design (describe):

Illustrations (describe):

Print type and size:

14. **EFFICIENCY QUOTIENT**

Cost vs. skills, concepts presented.

How many students can participate at one time?

Required teacher involvement?

How much time is required by the student?

______ Consumable ______ Reusable

15. **FIELD TEST DATA**

_______ In manual or guide _______ Available on request

_______ None given or available

Quality of data:

_______ High

_______ Average

_______ Poor

Comment: ____

____

16. **RESEARCH DATA**

_______ In manual or guide _______ Available on request

_______ None given or available

Quality of data:

_______ High

_______ Average

_______ Poor

Comment: ____

____

____

Larsen and Poplin (1980, pp. 362-366) cite Brown's Q-Sheet (1975, pp. 15-17) as one of the most extensive materials analyses available to special educators. Their abridged Q-Sheet is presented below.

Q-SHEET

1. What is the stated rationale for developing the program?

   Look for one or more statements of: (a) definition of the content area under study, e.g., reading; (b) philosophy regarding instruction in the area; or (c) dissatisfaction with specific aspects of other programs, or perhaps a previous program by the same publisher.

2. What is the rationale for selection of program elements or content?

   Look for comments on: (a) tradition; (b) experimental determination (always check this out in greater detail); (c) logic of the subject matter; (d) survey of other programs and their elements; or (e) the assumptions made concerning the content area, such as the linguistic base in a reading program.

3. How can the quality of the content be checked?

   This question is difficult. Usually some credence is given to the reputations of authors and publishers, as well as to supporting reference material. Usually "expert" opinion is needed in addition to a determination of the internal consistency of all program elements.

4. What is the scope of the program?

   Scope is the comprehensiveness or the breadth of the program. It determines how much of what it is possible to teach has been included in the program at hand. A program of limited scope may be desireable for teaching a specific skill, or as a supplement to an existing program which is weak in a particular area or variable.

5. What is the sequencing of skills or items or units?

   Sequence is the order in which the subject matter or elements are to be taught. Some materials are sequentially dependent so that mastery at each level is required before continuing to the next. Sequentially dependent curricula leave little room for flexible use or the pulling out of components. Other materials are "spiralled" so that the topic may be left and then returned to later. Paradoxically, spiralling may be helpful or detrimental. Sometimes leaving an area of difficulty for a while has the effect of desensitization. However, it may also be possible that mastery is never actually accounted for in a spiralled curriculum except when the particular topic disappears from "mention." Sequence may also be based upon several factors other than the sequential/spiral question. Logical organization of the subject matter may be a determiner; the curriculum may proceed from immediate to remote life experiences, or it may move from concrete to abstract symbolism.

6. How is the curriculum paced?

   Regulation of pacing is presently one of the major ways of controlling individualization of instruction. Several bits of information provide clues to intended and actual pacing of the materials or program:

   a. Are there differing starting times for various groups or individuals, and then essentially the same pacing along the way? If so, the modification is not in "pacing" but in readiness for the program.

   b. Are "mastery" suggestions made along the way for those who need more or different experiences at various points? How is it suggested that such modifications be managed if in a group situation?

   c. Do suggested instructional time lines presented elsewhere in the program mitigate against modifications in the pacing of instruction?

7. Is there evidence of any psychological principles of instruction which are content-free?

8. What are the specific techniques of instruction for each lesson?

   The more highly structured the lessons, the less likely it is that the success of the program depends upon the teacher experience and previous training. More highly structured programs also lend themselves to use by aides and volunteers under the supervision of the teacher. On the other hand, it may happen that if little teacher variation is allowed or encouraged, the lesson may not be readily modifiable.

9. What are the specific modifications suggested for individualization?

   a. Is the individualization on a one-to-one basis, or intended for instruction within the group situation?

b. What are the bases for the suggestions made?

c. What is the range of suggestions or are they all pretty much alike?

d. What range of differences is accounted for?

e. Are the suggestions general, or are they specifically tied to potential instructional problems?

10. Is a prerequisite skill level or information base needed to administer the program?

a. Is there a formalized, separate "package" of instruction available?

b. Is the training continuous as an integral part of each unit or lesson?

c. Are there ways to determine the instructional competency of personnel who would work with the program?

11. Are there "readiness" behaviors specified which are prerequisites for the student?

a. Are assessment strategies included?

b. How are the behaviors to be acquired or taught?

12. How is reinforcement used in the program?

a. If mentioned at all, note the definition well. In the majority of nonspecial education programs there is a tendency to equate reinforcement with repetition.

b. What kinds of reinforcement are suggested, e.g., social, tangible, edible, visual. . .?

c. Are there suggestions for how to determine what is reinforcing to an individual child?

d. Are schedules of reinforcement considered?

e. Are there specific examples, or generalized suggestions?

f. Is there a procedure for fading from tangible to social reinforcement?

g. Is there any discrepancy between notions of reinforcement and practices such as paper-grading or marking?

13. What is the format of the material to be presented?

a. Is the material in kit, book, worksheet, chart or some other form?

b. How are the units organized?

c. What kind of type is used? Size? Style? Compactness?

d. If pictures are included, what kinds are there, and what are their purposes?

e. Are the page arrangements likely to make any difference to the learners?

14. How independently can the material be used?

a. If independence of use is recommended, is there a systematic program to teach the child how to use the materials independently?

b. How is progress in work habits or independence to be monitored?

15. Has any effort been made to assess or control the complexity of the language of instruction, either receptively or expressively?

16. What is the developmental interest level of the materials?

Materials which are obivously intended for younger children are probably inappropriate for older students. On the other hand, the teacher actually may have to develop or provide background experience, information or interests for some students. It should be noted that statements of "mental age" do not necessarily correspond to the "interest age" or to the "social age" of the child.

17. Are there behavioral objectives for the program or for the lesson?

a. Is there any attempt to justify the objectives or to determine their value?

b. Are the objectives linked in any way to prior or to subsequent objectives?

c. Are the statements complete in the sense of meeting behavioral criteria?

d. What are the consequences of objectives assessment in terms of furture instructional procedures?

e. Is the program built on predetermined objectives, or do the objectives follow the nature of the program?

18. What diagnostic assessments are provided?

a. Type

b. Frequency?

c. Pre/post, or continuous during instructional sequences?

d. Feedback mechanisms to the learner and to the instructional program?

e. What are the consequences of assessment feedback?

19. Is this program coordinated with any other program?

a. Is the program part of a series or a unified approach by the same publisher? Can it be readily separated from other components?

b. Are there recommendations for companion programs, or for previous and subsequent programs?

20. Have there been any attempts to determine readability or learner interest?

What processess have been used, and are the results available?

21. What is the comparative cost of the program?

22. What is the realistic availability of the instructional components?

23. Are testimonials, research, author claims, and published claims clearly differentiated?

a. Evidence of formative evaluation?

b. Evidence of summative evaluation?

c. Is there congruence between the program objectives and activities?

d. Are the program development processes specified?

24. What are the target populations for whom the materials were developed?

If the population characteristics are stated, it is easier to assess the potential relevance of the materials to your population of interest.

25. Is it possible to foresee — and does the author note — any potential problems which might be encountered in using these materials?

a. How surmountable are the problems?

b. How readily can the materials be modified to resolve the problems?

26. Can any of the features of this material or program be adapted or incorporated into other programs?

    Features such as self-correctional procedures, reinforcement techniques, etc., may be noted for use in other instructional situations.

27. Are any significant changes in the organization and management of the institutional situation required?

    a. Are there special space and/or equipment requirements?

    b. Will the time/event schedule of the day need to be replanned?

    c. Will present child groupings be significantly affected? How?

    d. Are the descriptions of how the program is to be organized and managed stated clearly enough so that the program may be readily implemented?

28. Is it possible to isolate sensory channels as a major instructional variable?

    Keep in mind that for this purpose not only must the material itself be examined, but also the circumstances surrounding its actual presentation in the instructional situation.

29. How durable are the materials?

    Items that undergo a great deal of handling should be made of strong materials with protected surfaces. Storage or carrying of materials in kits or package form should also be considered in terms of the convenience and sturdiness of the packaging materials.

30. Is there any apparent or subtle bias toward or against a particular target group, e.g., women, blacks, Chicanos, or Indians?

    Many states or local school districts will have guidelines available for this kind of analysis.

31. Other significant features omitted from this list but which should be noted as relevant for user purposes.

    Considerations such as potential interaction patterns, the predominance of convergent/divergent responses, or detailed linguistic analysis may be of interest to special interest users.

Some materials analysis formats are specific to content or subject areas. For example, Fry (1977, pp. 148-149) provides a series of questions that teachers should respond to when selecting reading materials. They are divided into sections to be considered and are as follows:

INTEREST

Would the story content interest the pupils?

Are the activities interesting?

Are the artwork and illustrations relevant, artistic, and not offensive to any group?

SKILLS

Compare the phonics, work-attack, and comprehensive skills with several other lists that you like.

Are higher skills taught, such as speed, study skills, reference? (Use several lists.)

One way of finding out which skills are taught is to look at the scope and sequence chart, but you must then look at the teacher's manuals to see if the skills listed on the scope and sequence chart can really be found in the teacher's manuals and workbooks in the proper amount and that they are taught in a meaningful and worthwhile fashion.

LITERARY MERIT

Are the stories and poems good?

Are the students put in touch with good children's literature — either in the books themselves or in suggested activities?

Is there a good variety of material type?

TEACHABILITY

Are the teacher's directions clear and useful?

Is the material organized so that there is little confusion?

Can the children use the materials without an overdependence on the teacher?

Would the children really learn if the directions were followed?

Are there useful supplementary materials?

RANGE OF STUDENT ACTIVITIES

Does the system provide adequately for the type of students in your school?

Does it provide for individual differences?

Is the readability of the stories on the right level? (Don't just take the publisher's word for this; use a readability formula and/or try it out on some typical students.)

Does it provide for students who fail or need extra help?

EVALUATION

Do the teacher's manuals, workbooks, and other materials provide for frequent and accurate feedback on the student's progress?

Are there more formal testing programs either as separate tests or as part of drill activities?

Is there any record-keeping system for progress?

AUTHORSHIP AND PUBLISHER

Are the authors known and respected in the reading field?

Does the publisher have a good reputation for quality, content, service, and durability of materials?

COSTS

What is the initial (first-year) cost?

What is the replacement cost (second-year or five-year cost)?

How does the cost compare with similar systems?

Even if it costs more, is it worth it?

EFFECTIVENESS

Is there any evidence (journal articles, reports, etc.) that the series does indeed teach reading?

Can you visit other schools using the series, talk to teachers, see test results?

It appears that the questions formulated by Fry (1977) could be adapted or modified for other areas of the curriculum. And although this list is not as structured as the forms by Watson and Van Etten (1976) and Brown (1975), it clearly achieves the purpose of materials analysis, that is, to evaluate instructional materials in a thoughtful, systematic fashion.

Resources for Instructional Materials

Resource room teachers should note that most publishers of educational materials send their products for a thirty- to sixty-day review period. By reviewing materials throughout the school year, one can begin an orderly process of selection for the following year, rather than scramble through catalogues at budget time. Information is also available from various materials information sources. Stowitschek, Gable, and Hendricksen (1980, pp. 51-55) compiled the information listed below.

NCEMMH

Organization Name

National Center for Education Media and Materials for the Handicapped.

Stated Goal

The goal of NCEMMH is to assist and support personnel working with the handicapped in choosing and locating educational materials and media.

What It Is

It is a national center to help regions, states, and localities provide media, materials, and educational technologies. The center consists of four parts:

1. Media, Materials, and Technology (MMT), which facilitates the distribution of instructional and training materials;
2. Information Services (IS), which deals in information retrieval (see separate section on NIMIS);
3. Coordination Services (CS), which sees that all parts operate together; and
4. Administration and Central Technical Services (ACTS), which administers to the whole.

Who Can Use It

It is available to handicapped learners, teachers (public and private), parents, school administrators, librarians, media specialists, resource center personnel, medical center staff, rehabilitation center staff, researchers, and preservice teachers in special education programs.

How to Use It

Order materials and media in the NCEMMH catalogue directly from the manufacturer. Call Information Services (IS) for information not covered in the catalogue. Order other catalogues and in-house publications from the Ohio State University Press.

Costs

Catalogue and services are free; publications are available at a modest price.

NIMIS I

Organization Name

National Instructional Materials Information System (NIMIS I). NIMIS I is a subcomponent of NCEMMH.

Function

The function is to provide abstracts of materials and media from a data base. These abstracts are designed to aid in a search for appropriate materials when designing individualized education programs (IEPs).

Form

Thirty-seven abstracts are accessible through 41 hard-bound bibliographies divided into seven areas: Learning Disabilities, Early Childhood, Mildly Handicapped, Trainable Mentally Handicapped, Severely Mentally Handicapped, Hearing Impaired, and other topics. A computer printout may also be ordered.

Additional Publications

NIMIS Data Preparation Manual (approximately $6), *Instructional Materials Thesaurus for Special Education* (approximately $7). Note: New Service — Special Materials Analysis and Review by Teachers (SMART). Teachers provide information on materials they have used for possible entry into NIMIS I.

Prices

Individual abstracts (approximately $3-$5; entire set of abstracts (approximately $162); computer services (prices vary according to services).

Contact

Publications Sales Divisions, Ohio State University Press, 2070 Neil Avenue, Columbus, OH 43210.

NICSEM

Organization Name

National Information Center for Special Education Materials.

Function

The function of NICSEM is to aid in the search for appropriate materials by collecting abstracts from a data base along parameters defined by key words.

Forms

Numerous indexes are offered for sale (see NICSEM for a complete lists). A computer search is also available through NICSEM. There is an on-line interface with Lockheed (DIALOG) and BRS systems. Over 80,000 abstracts are available.

Prices

Index prices are quoted under NICSEM section. On-line computer service prices vary with the type of service.

Note: NICSEM is currently working to assist state education agencies in preparing and utilizing NICSEM products and services in their respective states.

Where to Order Indexes

University of Southern California, NICSEM, University (RAN) 2nd Floor, Los Angeles, CA 90007, Information Officer (213) 741-5899.

HLMDC

Organization Name

Handicapped Learner Materials Distribution Center.

Stated Goals

The goals of the HLMDC are to serve as a backup source in the event that materials are otherwise inavailable for loan. Materials may be used for evaluation for possible purchase or for actual use.

What It Is

It is a storehouse of materials for use with handicapped learners. Materials are accessible through catalogue orders for short-term loans.

Who Can Use It

Any organization, institution, or agency working with the handicapped or training workers with the handicapped can use it. Also, it can be used by parents of a handicapped child.

How to Use It

1. Determine the materials desired; the materials must be unavailable through local loan services.
2. Order them by mail, phone, or in person (a three-week notice is preferred).
3. Use the materials for one to seven days (longer loans are available on request).
4. Return the materials to HLMDS (the user is responsible for return postage).

Cost

There is no charge for loans. A catalogue is available upon request. Note: The user does accept responsibility for the condition of the material as returned to the HLMDC. Extensive guidelines are listed in the catalogue and the newsletter (vol. 1, no. 1, 1979) available from HLMDC.

How to Order Materials

1. Obtain a catalogue from Handicapped Learner Materials Distribution Center, Indiana University, Audio-Visual Center, Bloomington, Indiana 47405, (812) 337-1511 — Circulation Department.
2. Obtain a HLMDC account number at the same address and phone number.
3. Order needed materials three weeks in advance (some orders may be handled faster if phoned).
4. Return materials to HLMDC (the user pays return postage).

It is also wise to inquire about the availability of materials for loan or review through one's own state's special education office. Many states have regional or local centers that can be useful sources of materials. A phone call or letter of inquiry may yield a wealth of "free" materials.

A word of caution. Although there are many free instructional materials available for special education resource room teachers, one must be careful not to get swept away with kits and programs that purport to solve all problems. The most important set of materials that resource room teachers have available to them are those used in the regular education setting. By carefully adapting and modifying these materials, students will be better prepared for mainstreamed instruction. Materials selection should be based on meeting a particular objective (or set of objectives) with a student. When the materials start to dictate planning and instruction, the gap between expectation and performance will widen.

3

Programming

ACADEMIC PROGRAMMING

Students are placed in special education resource rooms when they exhibit academic or behavioral deficiencies that produce failure in regular classroom settings. These deficiencies are not so severe that they warrant a special self-contained classroom, and yet they clearly interfere with school success. The resource room program must be developed to reduce, if not eliminate, these difficulties. More to the point, Anderson-Inman (1986) states that "if the instructional support provided in pull-out settings such as resource rooms does not result in improved regular class performance, then the resource room instruction has not been successful" (p. 563). Given this theoretical assumption, the focus of the academic program developed and implemented by the resource room teacher must be on the transfer of skills taught in the resource room to the regular classroom. The resource room teacher must continually monitor the academic performance of his or her students in order to ascertain whether or not the instruction in the resource room is successful. It is simply insufficient to employ standard special education methods and materials in the resource room if such procedures fail to yield successful results in the regular classroom. This need to teach for transfer represents a radical shift in instruction for many resource room teachers and will force some to hide behind the shield of blaming regular educators for the failure of special education students. Alternately, it will enable some resource room teachers to become more aware of the goals of regular education and the need to be more cognizant of the wide variety of approaches that are applied in regular classroom settings. The challenge is to develop academic programs that will enable the special education student to succeed in the regular classroom while still being aware of the need for specialized instruction. Successful resource room teachers are always aware of the activities of the regular classroom. They keep informed by consulting (see chapter 4), reviewing the lesson plan of the regular educator, and discussing the content with the resource room students. Without this awareness they would not be able to monitor the success of their students.

The IEP and Academic Programming

Frequently the IEP (individualized education program) is written by the resource room teacher; however, even if it is not, the resource room teacher must carry out an IEP that reflects the reality that students will spend most of their school day in mainstreamed settings. IEP goals that concentrate on processes such as auditory attention span, graphomotor skills, visual perception, and so forth fail to address those skills necessary for success in the regular classroom. Too often these process goals are gleaned from tests administered during the identification and placement stages and may have little bearing on the student's performance in the classroom. For example, recently a science teacher queried a resource room teacher about the "auditory attention span deficit" of one of their students. The resource room teacher could only relate this deficit to the test results and could not apply it to the performance this teacher may or may not expect to see in his regular science class. To be sure, if this student is to do well in science, the resource room teacher must be cognizant of the goals, objectives, and activities of the science class and be equally aware of the student's learning strengths and weaknesses and develop a program that reflects these two components.

Deno and Mirkin (1980, p. 93) have developed a fairly comprehensive data-based approach to IEP development that addresses the concerns noted above. The model (Data-Based Program Modification) allows for a systematic evaluation of each of the concerns addressed on the student's IEP. The IEP is developed and modified by moving through the areas noted below:

Decision Area (Question)

Problem Selection

What are the problems that provided impetus for the referral and imply the need for program modification and special education service?

Data-Gathering Process

Initial Needs Assessment

1. Determine who holds performance expectations for the child.
2. Measure the current level and direction of the child's performance.
3. Graph the discrepancy between performance expectations and the child's actual level of performance.
4. Establish the importance rating (value) of the discrepancy.

Program Selection

What program plan is likely to be least restrictive and yet effective in solving the referrer's problem(s)?

Program Planning

1. Develop possible long- and short-range instructional goals for each discrepancy.
2. Plan alternative instructional strategies for achieving the goals.
3. Recommend alternative administrative arrangements.
4. Estimate time and resources necessary for attaining different goals using different modifications.
5. Specify forces working for or against different modifications.

Program Operationalization

Is the agreed-upon program modification being implemented as planned?

Implementation Evaluation (Intervention)

1. Appraise discrepancy between implemented program and planned program.
2. Ascertain reasons for discrepancy if they exist.
3. Propose alternative ways to reduce discrepancy between planned and implemented program.

Program Improvement

Does the program modification as implemented appear to be moving us to problem solution?

Progress Evaluation (Intervention)

1. Appraise progress on short- and long-range objectives.
2. Propose alternative revisions for programs that are not improving performance.

Program Certification

Were the problem(s) solved through program modification (intervention)?

Outcome Evaluation (Nonintervention)

Determine whether program modifications have been successful in eliminating the discrepancies that led to initial referral.

Although this type of activity is time-consuming, it is time well spent because it enables the resource room teacher to guard against irrelevant goals and objectives that will not facilitate improvement in the regular classroom. A more detailed analysis of this model can be found in Deno and Merkin (1977).

Elementary Grades

Academic programming in the elementary resource room must provide students with the basic skills that will enable them to succeed in school. Their goals are no different than the goals of all students; however, the means employed to attain them may differ markedly. In general, intervention strategies should begin with the least amount of variation from traditional methodology and should move toward more specialized approaches based on student's needs. This tactic facilitates transfer and allows the regular educator to reinforce activities employed in the resource room. It is not meant to suggest that if a student's needs are such that a highly specialized approach is warranted that it should not be used; it is only meant as a caution against using techniques that may not be necessary. Resource room teachers and their regular education counterparts must recognize that the size of the resource room group or individualized instruction, the type and frequency of reinforcement, and the pacing of instruction are also variables to be considered when developing an academic program. The major areas that must be addressed are reading, handwriting, spelling, written language, and mathematics. As students move through the elementary grades, content areas (science and social studies) are introduced and may pose a special problem for the mildly disabled student who is placed in the resource room.

Reading Instruction. Because reading is crucial for school success, it is not surprising that there is a wealth of information on ways to intervene when reading is not proceeding at an expected rate. Typically, reading instruction proceeds uneventfully for the large majority of schoolchildren. They are usually taught, using a basal reading program or a reading series. These programs generally fall into one of six general approaches to reading, as described by Smith (1983, pp.439, 440, 441). The six approaches are presented below. Included are the cautions that should be exercised when working with learning disabled students. It appears that these cautions also apply to most students who are placed in resource rooms.

Approaches to Reading Instruction

and

Cautions with Respect to LD Students

1. Visual Approaches

Visual methods are often referred to as "look-say" because words are taught by visual discrimination of letters and remembering what several letters grouped together look like. The contours of the words are highlighted in order to help children distinguish and remember them.

CORN POND KITE

Many basal readers (graded series developed for the average reader) incorporate a visual approach in beginning reading (e.g., *Scott Foresman*). Eventually decoding skills are added. Comprehension is emphasized throughout.

Caution

The visual approach encourages the poor reader's impulsive "look-guess" strategies. Most children will deduce phonetic rules when they have learned enough words, but poor readers won't.

2. The Phonics Approach

The phonics method teaches children to associate printed letters with their corresponding sounds. Children can then use these phonic skills to analyze sound sequences, blend them together, and pronounce new words. "Pond" will be sounded out (pu — ah — nn — di) and then blended together again. A variety of reading series emphasize the phonic method (e.g., Engelmann and "Bruner's (1969) *Distar* program, Open Court, Ginn, Lippincott Publishers). Supplemental programs emphasizing phonics skills are a useful adjunct to any program (e.g., Spaldings, *The Writing Road to Reading*). Other published programs combine the phonetic and visual approaches (e.g., *The Phonovisual Method*; Schoolfield and Timberlake, 1960).

Caution

The phonic method will be difficult for the child who has trouble discriminating among sounds and initial and terminal letter sounds, blending sounds into words, or remembering the sounds of letters and words. . . .

Phonics will be difficult for the child who takes so long to retrieve one sound that the previous ones are forgotten.

3. The Linguistic Approach

Linguistic theorists emphasize the strong relationship between printed words and the reader's oral language skills. Since meaning precedes the printed word, and individual sounds don't occur in oral language (there is no real word such as "pu — ah — nn — di"), the linguistic method tries to shortcut combining letters to yield words, so that the reader can concentrate on meaning. . . . Once the student has learned to decode, reading for meaning can take place (Glass, 1973).

In a way, the linguistic approach combines visual and phonic methods. Word stems like "at" and "ick" are taught as sight words and then individual sounds are substituted at the beginning of the stem: *pat, rat, cat; pick, kick, sick.* Stems are taught that can be placed at the beginning (e.g., un, dis), end, or middle of words. There is a definite sequence to the presentation of words, regular spelling patterns first, followed by irregular forms. . . .

Caution

Some programs assume that the reader will be able to independently discover the relationship between the sound and the letter; this link may be difficult for the disabled reader.

Although this system has the advantages of using visual analysis while reducing the phonetic load, students may still be overloaded by having to learn too many sounds at once . . . .

4. Language Experience Methods

The language experience method emphasizes comprehension because the child's language is the foundation upon which reading skills are built . . . . The child uses his vocabulary to orally relate personal experiences. The teacher writes these on wall charts. If the child can answer meaningful questions about his story, he is directed to look at the individual words and letters and try to remember them. Activities such as illustrating, editing, and making permanent charts or books are encouraged. This approach encourages creativity, motivation for learning to read, and aids speaking, listening, spelling, and writing skills . . .

Caution

Though capitalizing on visual processing, motivation, and reading for meaning, it is unlikely that LD students will discover sound-symbol relationships for themselves.

The variety of words that need to be read and remembered may be confusing.

Most LD students need a systematic approach to phonics instruction.

5. Personalized Reading Approach

The personalized reading approach has been adopted by many alternative schools that wish children to read what is most meaningful to them. The goal is to erase the stigma of being behind everyone else that comes from being assigned to the "Blue Bird" graded reading group instead of the "Hawks." It represents a much broader way of thinking about reading than other approaches . . . .

The student chooses material which is of personal interest (books, magazines, newspapers) and reads at his or her own rate. It is highly motivating for students to participate in this type of independent approach.

Caution

Teachers must engage in systematic and continuous review because the LD reader may be "getting in over his head."

Subtle difficulties could go undetected and cause the student great difficulty later on.

The student may be denied opportunities for learning what is important to other schools and, if transferring schools or taking national competency tests, may fail (e.g., comprehension and compositon skills, grammatical analysis).

6. Programmed Instruction

Programmed instruction materials are the most extreme behaviorally oriented materials. They allow the student to be actively involved in learning and to progress at his or her own rate. The teacher is merely a guide. Programmed materials are presented in small sequential steps. The reader gets immediate feedback about whether or not the answers are correct, and then engages in additional examples of those skills in which he needs further practice.

Caution

The lack of presentation of material in small steps and constant review may compound the LD child's learning difficulties and reinforce learning of errors.

LD students usually need active teacher guidance and feedback; they cannot take independent initiative for learning, self-pacing, and self-correcting.

LD students usually need teacher checks on learning; they may be using the wrong cues for learning and find it easy to copy answers rather than problem-solving independently.

The resource room teacher should become familiar with the general approach employed in the school. The teacher should study the scope and sequence chart for the particular series used in order to become familiar with grade level expectations. If, for example, the short vowel "a" is taught in the middle of grade 1 and a resource room student in grade 2 still has not mastered it, the resource room teacher must list this as one priority. As always, it is wise to talk to the regular classroom teacher to ascertain whether he or she is deviating from the sequence of skills being taught. For most students attending the resource room, a combination of approaches may be necessary (Gearheart, 1985). There is no approach that is applicable to all mildly disabled readers; rather, the effective resource room teacher develops a package that matches the reading approach to the student's learning strengths with appropriate modifications. Dramatic modifications such as specialized alphabets and approaches are more restrictive in nature and are probably geared more toward special self-contained class instruction. In the resource room these should be thought of as a last resort. Specific information on specialized or "clinical" approaches can be found in Mercer and Mercer (1985), Myers and Hammill (1976), and Siegel and Gold (1982).

What follows are guidelines that should govern the instruction of reading in the resource room:

1. Follow the regular reading program, with modifications, to the maximum extent possible.
2. Spend time reading. Too often disabled readers avoid reading at all costs, and research indicates that increased time spent on task in reading will yield favorable results (Smith, 1983).

3. Do not engage in oral reading other than for diagnostic purposes. Choppy, disfluent reading will be reinforced by poor readers performing this unnecessary task.
4. Read aloud to the students. This provides them with a good reading "model," and also develops a large fund of information.
5. Provide a wide variety of language-based activities to enhance the student's experiential background and their level of comfort with the "language" of reading.
6. Use reading games to teach and reteach basic skills. See Mercer and Mercer (1985) for an extensive listing of such activities. To reiterate, there is no single approach that has been found to "cure" reading disorders. Students attending the resource room will usually not require major modifications in the reading program. More often, they will need to have the reading program modified in such a way that it is compatible with their learning strengths. Resource room teachers need to apply the least restrictive approach toward reading instruction. Therefore, a minor change in instruction can yield positive results. If a student is taught through a phonics-based approach in the regular classroom but is unsuccessful because he or she can't recall individual letter sounds, perhaps an approach that focuses on larger units, such as phonograms or the whole word, may be more effective. This ability to match instruction with the student's learning strengths is the key to good teaching — not just in the area of reading, but throughout the curriculum.

Successful Resource Room Teachers

1. Identify the reading approach employed in the regular classroom.
2. Get a set of materials.
3. Develop a curriculum-based assessment (see chapter 2).
4. Identify areas of need.
5. Develop and implement an instructional plan.
6. Evaluate results in the resource room.
7. Evaluate results in the regular classroom.
8. Make necessary modifications.
9. Repeat steps 5-7.

Spelling Instruction. If a student is experiencing difficulty in reading, there is a high probability that spelling difficulty will occur. There are also students who have spelling disorders with no concomitant reading disorder. Spelling is a complex task. Too often, however, it is reduced to memorizing word lists with little or no relationship to other language arts areas, in particular, reading. Resource room teachers must select spelling words that are relevant to instruction. These can come from reading lists, actual stories in the reading series, or content area material. The approach employed should reflect that used in reading instruction. For example, if the approach toward reading is primarily phonics, then it would follow that the spelling instruction would be phonics oriented. Children who have spelling difficulty usually do not have a systematic approach toward the task. Therefore, if they can be taught the interrelatedness of all areas of language arts and how to employ similar strategies, their chances for success will be enchanced. Once again, being aware of the spelling program used in the particular regular classroom will be of assistance when developing the spelling program in the resource room. Below are some effective and ineffective spelling methods (taken from Vallecorsa, A.L., Zigmond, N. and Henderson, L.M. (1985). Spelling instruction in special education classrooms: A survey of practices. *Exceptional Children*, *52*, 1, 19-24).

Effective Methods

Using a test-study-test procedure

Testing a few words daily

Using high-interest activities and motivational games

Emphasizing a core of high-frequency words first

Teaching words which are part of a student's listening and speaking vocabulary

Teaching strategies for whole-word study

Having students correct their own spelling work under the teacher's direction

Using a variety of remedial techniques rather than one approach

Developing students' dictionary skills

Frequently reevaluating words studied

Limited phonics instruction in teaching spelling

Developing students' proofreading skills

Presenting words in a list initially

Ineffective Methods

Using a test-study approach

Presenting words in sentences or paragraphs initially

Having students write words in the air to aid retention

Relying on commercial materials as foundation of the spelling program

Emphasizing spelling rules and generalizations

Permitting students to devise their own methods for studying spelling words

Using a synthetic alphabet

Having students write words several times to aid retention

Having students study "hard spots" in words

What does the resource room teacher do if the "ineffective methods" are those employed in the regular classroom? He or she must remember that the goals should be the same, but the methodology used to reach those goals may (and usually is) somewhat different. Many resource room teachers are faced with students who must write their misspelled words ten times each or memorize spelling rules or write words in the air while in their regular classroom. Gradually these teachers can change this type of ineffective instruction, but initially a simple remedy is to provide the spelling instruction in the resource room. Once success has been demonstrated, there is a better chance that the regular classroom teacher will change some of the ineffective techniques. As always, the goal is to increase performance in the regular classroom. The line between direct instruction (spelling) and indirect instruction (working with colleagues) is not often as clear in practice as it is in theory.

Handwriting Instruction. Graham and Miller (1980) discuss issues and practices surrounding the instruction of handwriting. They note two causes of handwriting problems: (1) a learner may bring to the classroom certain characteristics that impede effective instruction, and (2) poor instruction. They feel that the latter is a more viable causal factor and cite a number of studies that indicate that classroom teachers either do not know how to, or perfer not to, instruct students in this very important area of the curriculum. As a result of this concern, they have developed a model which represents a valuable approach for resource room teachers to consider (Graham and Miller, 1980, p. 5). The major objective of the handwriting model is to develop efficient, legible writers. To meet this goal, an effective program should be based on the following principles and conditions:

1. Handwriting instruction is direct and not incidental.
2. Because handicapped students exhibit a diverse range of handwriting achievement, instruction is individualized.
3. The handwriting program is planned, monitored, and modified on the basis of assessment information.
4. Successful teaching and remediation depend upon the flexible use of a wide variety of techniques and methods.
5. Handwriting is taught in short daily learning periods during which desirable habits are established.
6. Skills in handwriting are overlearned in isolation and then applied in meaningful context assignments.
7. Teachers stress the importance of handwriting and do not accept, condone, or encourage slovenly work.
8. Effective handwriting instruction is dependent upon the attitudes of both student and teacher.

9. The instructional atmosphere is pleasant, and motivation is promoted through incentives, reinforcement, success, and enthusiasm.
10. Teachers practice lessons prior to presentation and are able to write a "model" hand.
11. Students are encouraged to evaluate their own handwriting and, when appropriate, actively participate in initiating, conducting, and evaluating the remedial program.

Specifically, when students are learning to form letters, a combination of procedures can be employed:

Modeling. The teacher writes the letter and names it. The student observes.

Noting critical attributes. The teacher composes and contrasts the letter with similar letters.

Physical prompts and cues. The teacher physically directs the student's hand. Arrows, dots, and other color cues can also be used.

Tracing. The student traces dot-to-dot patterns, dashed letters, a faded model, raised letters, and/or an outline.

Copying. The student copies the letter on paper or wet sand.

Self-verbalization. The student says the steps to himself or herself.

Writing from memory. The student writes the letter without any cues.

Repetition. The student practices through multisensory drills.

Self-correction and feedback. The student corrects the letter through the use of an aid or teacher feedback.

Reinforcement. The student is praised for correct work.

The authors (Graham and Miller, 1980) also note that the teacher should observe the students to ensure that they are sitting properly, are holding the pencil or pen correctly, and have the paper on the correct angle.

The resource room program should supplement the handwriting program in the regular classroom. Monitoring the program's success will present it from becoming ineffective. It should be noted that if a student's handwriting is so illegible or if the rate is so slow and labored that it interferes with his or her ability to perform well on written assignments or tests, then the student should be provided with testing modifications, and specific indications of this problem should be included on the IEP.

Written Expression Instruction. Many resource room students will come running into the resource room and announce that they have to write an essay or report and yet have little ability to engage in such a complex task. And although there is considerable outcry regarding the lack of writing skills in the school-age population, it appears that mildly disabled students are far more severly disabled in this area of the curriculum than their nondisabled counterparts. Isaacson (1980, pp. 32-33) suggests that research findings lead to four general principles of effective writing instruction:

1. Allow sufficient time for writing instruction.
2. Track writing as a process.
3. Teach writing through interactive group experiences.
4. Avoid excessive use of corrective feedback.

Obviously, if written expression is to improve, it appears that many teachers need to rethink the manner in which this skill is taught. This is particularly true for the resource room teacher. The principles noted above can only be adhered to if the resource room teacher and the regular classroom teacher plan in a cooperative manner. They need to spend some part of each day engaged in the teaching of written expression. Many good resource room teachers allow for sufficient discussion prior to writing, but this approach may not be feasible in every regular classroom setting. Most good resource room teachers are well aware of the impact of corrective feedback on most mildly disabled students. However, unless these practices are carried out in both the regular and special setting, the probability that there will be observable gains in written expression will be low.

Resource room teachers and their regular education colleagues can work together in a number of ways. For example, if a written expression assignment is given to a special education student in the regular classroom, the resource room teacher can be notified. He or she can then provide for ample opportunity to discuss the topic, consider what will be written, and write, review, and revise the composition with the student or students.

Both teachers can provide positive verbal and nonverbal feedback and opportunities to practice in the resource room and the regular classroom. This type of interaction is critical if the written language skills of the mildly disabled learner are to improve.

Much has been written recently on teaching writing as a process. Many school districts are providing in-service courses for teachers, and conferences are held on a nationwide basis. Resource room teachers must become aware of these practices if they are being employed in their schools. A few excellent references that will provide a basic understanding of the writing process are *Learning by Teaching* (Murray, 1982); *Writing: Teachers and Children at Work* (Graves, 1983); and *The Art of Teaching Writing* (Calkins, 1986).

Johnson and Myklebust (1967, pp. 233-238) have developed a program to remediate written expressive language disorders. The major components of their approach are as follows:

1. *Concrete-Descriptive Stage.* The student describes what he or she sees — the here and now. Simple words and/or sentences are dictated to the teacher by the student and eventually written.
2. *Concrete-Imaginative Stage.* This stage requires the student to make an inference based on what he or she sees. Once again oral language precedes written language, so the student dictates, then writes.
3. *Abstract-Descriptive Stage.* This represents a major step because students are now required to be introduced to the notion of time, sequence, and written language sample that employ transition words and phrases.
4. *Abstract-Imaginative Stage.* This final stage requires the student to write a thorough composition.

Students may never reach the final stage or may take considerable time on the early stages. Teachers must remember that writing may be the most complex skill to teach and must proceed with realistic expectations. Ample oral discussion must be provided prior to writing. Throughout the teaching process teachers must provide a variety of experiences, direct instruction, opportunities to practice new skills, and a positive environment where red marks and sarcastic comments on papers are nonexistent. A more functional form of written expression is note taking. Polloway, Patton, and Cohen (1981, p. 13) list a few suggestions for teachers:

Note taking

1. Preparation
   a. Make sure all necessary materials are ready.

b. If available, obtain ahead of time a skeletal outline of the lecture from the teacher.

2. Instruction
   a. Give practice at taking notes.
   b. Provide feedback.
   c. Teach shorthand conventions, abbreviations, or personal codes (e.g., for without, for with).
   d. Emphasize that students are *not* to write down every word.
   e. Provide training in how to recognize key words ("most important") or key behaviors (listing on board or writing a key phrase on board) of teacher.

3. Aids
   a. Have students use small pocket-size notebooks for various tasks (assignments, "things to do today," questions for teacher).
   b. Encourage taping of lecture notes to augment note taking.
   c. Check notes with those of a good note taker.

Math Instruction. Very little information is available regarding instruction in math for mildly disabled students. Clearly, as in all other areas, the regular classroom curriculum should be examined. Much of what occurs under the heading of math remediation reflects a great deal of creativity on the part of the teacher. Typically, teachers will employ techniques that reduce the complexity of the task and that increase basic fact retention, organization of the algorithm, and focusing of the student's attention. Below is a list of interventions (from Siegel and Gold, 1982, pp. 242, 243, 244) for common math difficulties experienced by learning disabled students. They are equally useful for all students attending the resource room who experience math difficulty.

1a. *Guessing answers, implulsive responses.* Prevent impulsive responses rather than the number of items completed. Do not present many examples or problems at one time. Some children respond to "so much work" by racing through, trying to get it over quickly. For these children, withhold their pencil, while they think through the problem. For oral responses, encourage "thinking time," rather than speed of response.

1b. *Difficulty in completing work.* Many workbooks have too much material in them, causing distraction. For this child, too, fewer items should be presented at one time. A cardboard window can be used to frame each example or problem while blocking out the others on the page. Behavior modification techniques can also be helpful.

1c. *Repetition in writing numbers.* Some children tend to perseverate and continue writing a response beyond what is appropriate. This happens frequently when drilling in writing in numerals. Structure the assignment or page so that repetition will not be encouraged. Do not have the child write the numeral more than once before introducing another numeral.

1d. *Repeating a computational operation.* To prevent continuation of operations, alternate operations are required so that a pattern is not established. In some cases it may be necessary to alternate modes of responses or materials.

2a. *Auditory memory deficits.* Visual presentations can be linked with the auditory, so that the child is not limited by the weaker modality. The visual representation can be stressed.

2b. *Visual memory problems.* Children who have difficulty revisualizing numbers can learn to use verbal prompts or mediators. Some respond best if a motor cue is taught. Color cuing can sometimes be utilized. The process signs can be written in different colors. Problems can be given orally.

3a. *Dysgraphia.* When children have difficulty in writing numerals, alternatives must be considered. Writing should be kept to a minimum. Printed or duplicated materials can be used so that only answers need be filled in. In some cases, the child can be directed to underline the correct response from among three or four. A stamp pad and numeral stamps can be provided so that the child need only stamp in the correct answer. Answers can be given orally to the teacher or aide, or on a tape recorder.

3b. *Erasing difficulties.* This is a problem, though minor, which can adversely affect children's written performance. Frequently they do such a poor job that they cannot separate what was rewritten from what was erased. Another factor should also be considered. Some children are fearful of making errors. By teaching them how to erase an error, we are also saying that mistakes can be undone.

4a. *Difficulties distinguishing size, shapes, lengths, and/or amounts.* Provide a variety of real materials for comparison to arrange in order of size, length, weight, and so on. All senses should be utilized: touching, looking, counting aloud. Such activities can be done simultaneously with some children but with a single sensory approach with others. Stern blocks and pattern boards or Cuisinaire rods can be used to build trains and stairs so the children can compare size, lengths, and numerical combinations.

Concept words such as "heavy-light," "bigger-smaller" must be taught specifically. Things that go together related to size can be taught using cut-out dolls, photos, and so forth. Ask questions such as: "Which clothes will fit which doll?" "Which car is the right size for the garage?" Children also need experiences in weighing and measuring items. The child should initially learn to feel the difference between one pound and five pounds; then finer discriminations should be learned.

Puzzles and form boards provide clues to shapes. Discuss the shape needed to fill the space. Have the child feel and describe the shapes without looking at them. Many LD children have verbal strengths and these should be tapped in various learning situations (Johnson and Myklebust, 1967, p. 254). Large outlines of shapes can be placed on the floor. The children can trace the shapes as they walk along the edges.

4b. *Deficits in estimating time and/or chronological sequence.* Have the child estimate how long he thinks an activity will take. Have him show on a demonstration clock what it will look like when the time will be up. Compare the time on the demonstration clock with the actual time.

Using a timer and have the child attempt to complete a task before it rings. The teacher should integrate the use of time concepts in natural classroom situations: e.g., "We have five minutes to clean up before it is time to go to lunch."

To facilitate memory of sequence steps, verbal or visual cues can be used. Charts can show step-by-step procedures. Verbalizations should be clear and concise. This skill is important in learning to follow directions in a recipe but also in performing computations and in doing two- and three-step word problems.

4c. *Difficulties in maintaining columns.* Writing numerals in columns can be aided by providing a strong visual and possible tactile stimulus. The space for writing the examples can be set off by a heavy line or a raised barrier (cardboard frame). Colored lines on the paper can set off the place-value columns. Using ruled paper with the lines running vertically can also provide the needed structure. As proficiency is developed, the stimulus should be faded.

5a. *Orientation problems.* The concepts right-left, up-down, in-out, under-over, and so on should be used in real situations in the classroom and then applied to workbook or other two-dimensional planes. Because of the concrete thinking of many LD children, they have difficulty transferring concepts understood in the "real world" to the two-dimensional world of their texts and workbooks. Specific teaching of the relationship between the real and representational frequently has to be provided. Cues such as a color or a shape may be used to show directions. Arrows can be used to indicate the direction in which to work calculations or where to "carry."

Content Areas. Just when many mildly disabled students are beginning to develop a mastery of the basic skills, they are often introduced to the content areas of science and social studies. The resource room teacher must be aware of the ways in which learning problems manifest themselves in the content areas and develop modifications (in cooperation with the regular classroom teacher) to overcome these problems. Siegel and Gold (1983) have developed such a list of these problems and manifestations.

Science

	Pitfalls	*Modifications*
1.	The LD child may be uncoordinated: e.g., breaks glass beakers, cuts fingers while stripping wires.	Initially use plastic beakers (if possible); train in use of wire strippers (at first, use prestripped wire leads).
2.	The equipment, material, and apparatus may distract the impulsive, motor-disinhibited, fidgety child.	Clear his desk of extraneous material. Hand him one item at a time. Take out equipment only when it is needed; collect it all when the experiment is done.
3.	The LD pupil may become impressed with the "magic" aspect and miss the scientific priniciple.	Emphasize cause-effect relationships. Ask specific questions ("What do you think will happen if . . .?" "Why will it happen?"). Shulene (1975) developed a set of simple pictorial riddles — each picture focuses the child's attention upon a specific piece of scientific information. For example, one cartoon depicts a boy standing in a flooded basement reaching up to turn the switch on an overhead light. Questions such as "Can you tell me about other ways people receive electric shocks?" and "What do you think will make this a safer picture?" are asked.

	Pitfalls	*Modifications*
4.	He may "generalize" incorrectly: e.g., the teacher holds bare wires connected to a six-volt battery; later, the child inserts bare wires into electrical wall outlets.	Anticipate this style of thinking. Be one step ahead of the child, i.e., discuss the differences between a six-volt battery and a 110-volt line *before* the mistake.
5.	The LD pupil may not understand abstract terms and ideas.	Progress slowly, step by step. Concretize the lesson: use simple terms, models, pictures or real situations. Use many illustrations of the concept being taught.
6.	He may encounter difficulty reading the regular science text.	"Rewrite" the text in simple terms. Use pictures combined with small amounts of written material. Utilize high-interest-low-reading-level book.
7a.	Some LD children may lack exploratory drive and are overly dependent upon others in selecting areas of interests and activities (Hewett, 1968).	Use the strategies of (1) *forced-choice*, but from a small set of alternatives (no more than two or three of them); and/or (2) *first choice* (i.e., the child is invited to choose first, in deference to his tendency of merely falling in line with the others — provided of course that he is sufficiently strong emotionally (Hewett, 1968, pp. 190-191).
7b.	On the other extreme is the LD child who explores too much, but in a random, restless, erratic, purposeless and "driven" fashion.	Structure the lesson. The child needs direction. A brief discussion at the outset can focus upon the *reason* for the experiment, some of the events likely to occur, and effective practices to employ during this exploration. Teacher observations, support, and frequent questioning at strategic intervals help initially. Gradually, the reins can be loosened (Siegel and Gold, pp. 261-262).

Social Studies

1. The LD child may have difficulty with many of the abstract concepts and terms.	Emphasize those aspects of history and geography that deal with the child's immediate environment. Relate how people lived in the past or how they live in other countries to the child's life. Go a step further and personalize the lesson, alluding to some specifics regarding a particular pupil (e.g., refer to a child's after-school newspaper route, another child's recent trip to New Hampshire). Concretize by using similar terms, many examples, representative materials (e.g., a timeline to clarify temporal concepts), illustrations and analogies. Stress current events, current mores and topics of interest (sports, music, TV shows, dances). Utilize field trips, audio-visual aids, and guest speakers.
2. The LD pupil may be deficient in reading.	The same content can be found in books of different reading levels. An excellent example is the *The Silver Burdett Series*. . . The grade level is deliberately not specified, verbiage is sparse, there are many failure-free and success-assured activities. It contains many meaningful photographs. Use simple rexograph sheets instead of texts. Weiss and Weiss (1974) advise that the text of these sheets be simplified with some modification of the vocabulary. The print should be large type, all capital letters and well spaced. (They suggest the Orator type from an IBM Selectric Typewriter ball (pp. 73-78).

Social Studies

3. He may have deficits in writing (spelling and written composition as well as penmanship).	Reduce the number of written assignments. Accept written outlines initially in lieu of entire essays. Utilize the experience chart (wherein the pupil dictates his words and the teacher does the writing), oral reports, and the tape recorder. Some LD children, despite incoordination, can benefit by learning to type. There are some educators who have developed special methods for teaching typewriting to LD children: for example, Jack Heller's *How to Master Touch Typing* (Wantagh, N.Y.: Special Education, Step-By-Step, 1978).
4a. He may have poor listening skills. This may stem from such factors as distractibility, auditory imperception, restlessness.	Avoid lengthy lectures. Try to cut down on teacher verbiage and encourage more pupil-pupil interaction. Provide for physical movement: changing seats for committee purposes; going from one "center" to another — e.g., the "map corner" to the "graphs and charts table"; seat work interspersed with chalkboard activities. Also utilize manipulative activities — e.g., sorting, matching, collating.

Social Studies

4b. Many LD children find it difficult to take notes. This hinders them in secondary schools and can prove disastrous later in college. Very likely, taking notes constitutes a formidable task for LD children, particularly those prone to neurological overloading, for two reasons: (1) They must do two things at once — listen and write, and (2) there is a continuous lack of synchrony — they listen to the lecturer's *present* words, simultaneously writing about his *past* ones.

The most important way in which the teacher can help here is to be aware of the difficulty, thereby setting the stage for empathy rather than rejection to occur. The teacher should speak slower, not as much, and utilize handouts of the lecture in the beginning of the class. There can be actual training in note-taking skills. Hints such as use of abbreviations, underlining, and writing on every other line (thus allowing room for insertions) should be provided. The pupil should get systematic training in outlining initially. (Outlining is, in effect, a simpler form of note taking: in the former, one is asked to outline from visual stimuli — that is, the written text — whereas note taking is tantamount to outlining from auditory stimuli.) An excellent teaching aid in note taking is *Thirty Lessons in Note Taking* by Jenifer Pirie and Allex Pirie (Woburn, Mass.: Curriculum Associates, 1976).

4c. LD children may find instruction limited to visual and auditory modalities insufficient. It may be too unvaried, hence promoting boredom. Then, too, some LD children may be impaired in both of these areas.

Kelly (1979), in a book which devotes an entire chapter to the teaching of social studies in special education, suggests that teachers of LD children incorporate tactile and kinesthetic approaches when instructing them in social studies, e.g., flat maps with roadways having sandpaper surfaces; three-dimensional maps that have been deliberately distorted, thus facilitating the tactile examination of terrains; objects which can be handled, rubbed, and explored tactually.

Social Studies

5. The LD child may have problems in memory. This will hinder him in remembering historical facts: dates, people's names, the sequence of events. True, the sheer memorization of isolated facts should never be stressed. Of far greater importance are *concepts* such as motivations (of people and of governments) and interrelationships (of one event to another, of the individual to his country, of people to their environment). Nevertheless, inability to remember essential facts often detracts from mastery of the broader concepts.

   Avoid emphasizing memorization. Let the pupil feel free to look up data when needed; provide systematic instruction in the use of reference material. A timeline can help one visualize dates and avoid gross errors. Visual prompts can help. Songs (e.g., "The Erie Canal") and poems (e.g., "In Flanders Field"), although they do require memorization themselves, can promote the retaining of historical facts. Mnemonic devices can be useful: *M*ary *W*ants *C*old *N*oodles can cue the child to the relative spatial positions of *M*ontana, *W*yoming, *C*olorado, *N*ew *M*exico. Sometimes games and puzzles (e.g., simple map jigsaw puzzles) can facilitate tactile and kinesthetic memory.

6. Social Studies deals with broad outcomes (e.g., "to develop an awareness of our American Heritage," "to understand how the weather affects where and how people live") and hence does not lend itself handily to observable behavioral objectives. Because, with few exceptions (e.g., some discrete tasks in map skills, use of reference work, vocabulary building), social studies does not succumb to task analysis, it is difficult to teach (the teacher may wander, may try to cover too much, may not have any clear goals), difficult to learn, and difficult to measure the results of instruction.

   Use discrete, circumscribed topics. The fact that a topic which is broad in scope does not yield to task analysis need not prevent the teacher from subdividing it into a well-organized series of simpler concepts. The instructor should be systematic. Although one cannot often specify a definitive behavorial objective in social studies, it is possible — and necessary — to *plan* "an agenda," that is, an outline of exactly what ideas and facts will be covered in the lesson. The parts of the lesson should be required to participate actively (i.e., to *do* something). Appropriate materials should be selected. The pupil's past knowledge — that is, his *entering behavior* — should be taken into account. [pp. 130-135].

Any students placed in the resource room, whether they are classified as learning disabled, mentally retarded, or emotionally disturbed, may experience one or more of the problems noted above. The resource room teacher's awareness of the content area, the student's learning strengths, and ways to circumvent potential problems will greatly enhance the child's ability to succeed in science and social studies.

Secondary Grades

Academic programming in the secondary-level resource room requires a different orientation than was the case with the elementary grades. In addition to the considerable changes the typical adolescent is undergoing, the student with learning problems is faced with a widening gap between potential and achievement (Smith, 1983). There is also the realization that standard remedial approaches that were employed by resource room teachers on the elementary level are no longer appropriate on the secondary level (Alley and Deshler, 1979). The emphasis on the secondary level is to develop skills that apply to all content areas. Teachers must be aware that most students attending the resource room will only be doing so for one or two periods per day. For the remainder of the school day these students must be able to cope with the demands of the secondary school curriculum. As was the case on the elementary level, the resource room teacher must become aware of the requirements of the various content areas, as well as the way in which particular teachers approach their subject matter. This knowledge allows the resource room teacher to develop instructional plans that will be able to be transferred to the regular classroom setting. Students must be shown how a particular skill is applicable across settings, not merely useful in one content area. If we were to analyze those generic skills that are necessary across all content areas, develop academic programs that present these skills, and present them to students in such a way that they will be matched to the students' learning strengths, then students attending the resource room would have a fighting chance of succeeding in the mainstream. Unfortunately, this does not appear to take place in many secondary resource rooms, where students are able to get through the day be receiving tutoring, explanation of assignments and/or testing modification, but fail to receive instruction that will allow them to develop skills and strategies that will serve them in all of their classes — and beyond. What follows are instructional strategies that address these concerns.

Transenvironmental Programming. The essential elements of this approach are the acquisition of the skills necessary for success in the regular classroom and the transfer of these skills to mainstreamed settings (Anderson-Inman, 1986). The four major components are as follows:

1. *Environmental Assessment.* The resource room teacher must assess what is required in the regular classroom in order to develop an academic program. This assessment also allows the teacher to prioritize the skills to be taught so that there is a payoff in the content area classroom.
2. *Intreventional Preparation.* Anderson-Inman (1986) notes that "for resource room instruction to be most effective curriculum should focus on the specific skill identified as necessary for regular class success" (p. 564). This component concerns itself with the development of goals that are specific and germane to a particular content area, as opposed to general behavioral objectives.
3. *Promoting Transfer across Settings.* Student must employ their newly learned skills in the regular classroom environment. Strategies for transfer must be planned during and after instruction. Specific strategies will be described below.
4. *Evaluation in the Target Environment.* The purpose of this final component is to collect data that allows the resource room teacher to decide whether or not instruction in the resource room has been useful, that is, whether the student is succeeding in the regular classroom. Depending upon the evaluation, he or she may decide to continue the current approach or modify it.

Anderson-Inman (1986) and her colleagues at the University of Oregon feel that student input is essential if this approach is to succeed. She describes three student-centered transfer strategies that have been demonstrated to be effective in promoting the transfer of skills across settings. These can be employed in all resource rooms, but they appear to be especially useful on the secondary level. They are (1) student-requested preteaching; (2) curriculum-specific transfer training; and (3) self-monitoring checklists.

1. *Student-Requested Preteaching.* Initially the resource room teacher needs to consider the following variables: the subject matter, the instructional materials being used in the regular class, the regular class teacher's instructional style, and the student's current level of performance. Curriculum content and instructional format appear to be of particular importance in transferring skills. Resource room teachers should attempt to match the variables noted above and provide the students with "practice" in a skill before they have to perform the skill in the regular classroom. The author stresses

that student input is of critical importance in the selection of the skill or content area. She has found that the impact on performance in the regular class was the most successful when the student's wishes were respected. Students should also have significant input into the development of preteaching sessions. It appears that success in the regular classroom is a powerful reinforcer and that students are able to decide when they can succeed. The author also encourages students to keep their own records of their performances and make appropriate decisions based on the data.

2. *Curriculum-Specific Transfer Training.* Anderson-Inman and her colleagues have found that instruction in reading comprehension skills taught in the resource room does not automatically transfer to content area texts in regular classes. Therefore, they taught specific transfer strategies. Students must be taught the relationship between the activities in the resource room and those needed to do well in the regular class and should use the same regular classroom materials they are using in the content areas. Specifically, resource room teachers should do the following:

    a. Have a copy of content area texts in the resource room.
    b. Analyze each text for the most frequently required comprehension skills and prioritize the skills for each text. This should be done with considerable student input.
    c. Provide instruction in the particular skill using content area texts.
    d. Provide for guided practice in applying newly learned skills in a "simulated" regular classroom environment.

3. *Self-Monitoring Checklists.* A simple list of those skills necessary for success in the regular classroom can be developed by the resource room teacher and student. Students can monitor their own performance on a daily and/or weekly basis. These checklists enable students to focus on the particular skills they need to work on and can enable them to develop a sense of pride in their accomplishments because they are being made explicit. Anderson-Inman (1986) recommends that if the teacher decides to employ this strategy, he or she should (1) select those skills and behaviors that either "have occurred" or "have not occurred" to allow for simple record keeping; (2) build in a time for filling out the checklist; (3) start with one content area; and (4) monitor the procedures carefully. One final note — even if students are not accurate reporters of the day's events, it appears that the checklists are still effective.

Learning Strategies. This approach, developed at the University of Kansas Institute for Research in Learning Disabilities (KU-IRLD) (Alley and Deshler, 1979), teaches students "how to learn" so they can be effective learners in the secondary school. Deshler and Schumacher (1986) note that an example of the learning strategies approach would be a teacher who would instruct students in strategies for summarizing and managing material that has to be learned for social studies, rather then teach them the actual content of social studies. By doing so the teacher will develop strategies that can be used across the various content areas, not merely social studies. The learning strategies curriculum (Deshler and Schumacher, 1986) is organized in three major strands: (1) strategies that assist students in acquiring information for written materials; (2) strategies that enable students to identify and store important information; (3) strategies for facilitating written expression and demonstration of competence. These strands represent the expectations for secondary-level students in regular settings. The research team at KU-IRLD has developed an extensive list of specific strategies subsumed below the three major strands noted above, and interested practitioners can receive information by writing. Some of the major instructional principles of the KU-IRLD Learning Strategies Approach are as follows:

1. *Match instructor with curriculum demands.* The first step in this process is to understand exactly what types of curriculum demands the student is failing to meet (note taking, test taking, and so forth). This is a change of focus from assessment of student deficits to assessment of environmental demands. Academic programs are then developed to provide those strategies that will enable the student to succeed.
2. *Use structured teaching methodology.* The methodology employed in the learning strategy approach is as follows: (1) the student is assessed to determine his or her current learning habits regarding a particular task; (2) a new strategy is described to the student (component steps, rationale, results the student can expect, and situations when it can be used); (3) the new strategy is modeled for the student; (4) the student uses verbal rehearsal; (5) the student practices the new strategy in controlled materials (reduced in complexity, length, and difficulty level); (6) the student practices with material closely approximating that used in the regular classroom; and (7) the student performs the strategy in the regular setting and is evaluated.
3. *Deliberately promote generalization.* The researchers at KU-IRLD believe, as does Anderson-Inman (1986), that the "acid test" of resource room instruction is the degree to which the skill is generalized across settings and maintained over time. This is accomplished by (1) making students aware of the contexts in which

the strategy can be applied; (2) providing ample opportunity for practicing strategies in a wide variety of settings and with a variety of materials; and (3) providing periodic probes to ensure maintenance. The authors note that a cultural element in this process is the communication between regular and special educators.

4. *Apply "critical teaching" behavior.* These teaching behaviors are as follows:
    a. provide appropriate positive and corrective feedback
    b. Use organizers throughout instruction
    c. Ensure high levels of academic response
    d. Provide for youth involvement in discussions
    e. Provide regular reviews of key instructional points and checks of comprehension
    f. Monitor student performance
    g. Require mastery learning
    h. Communicate high expectations to students
    i. Communicate rationale for instructional activities
    j. Facilitate independence
5. *Use scope and sequence in teaching.* This is more of a plea than a guiding principle. It suggests that teachers need to plan a program over years if students are to become competent in a large number of strategies.
6. *Ensure that teaching decisions are governed by outcome goals.* Students must become aware of how they learn and of the realization that they have control over their own learning. By monitoring their progress in systematic fashion and evaluating programs by outcomes, the teacher can greatly facilitate this process.
7. *Maximize student involvement.* Simply stated, students must feel a sense of ownership in their academic program.
8. *Maintain realistic point-of-view.* The authors point out that not all students will benefit from this approach. Wise practitioners are aware that not all school failure on the secondary level can be attributed to a lack of appropriate learning strategies.

Metacognitive strategy instruction. Secondary-level resource room students need to be able to plan, implement, and evaluate strategic approaches to learning and problem solving. This approach allows students to assume control over their own learning (Palincsar, 1986). For successful metacognitive strategy instruction to occur, the following should be considered:

1. Critically evaluate strategies to determine how readily they can be taught and whether they are applicable across settings.

2. Provide students with information regarding the importance of the skill to be taught, when the skill is necessary, how to monitor their own progress, and how to apply the skill more readily. Students should also be provided with information about the reward for using such strategies.

3. Gradually transfer control of strategy from teacher to student.

4. Carefully select material so that it is representative of the material employed in the regular classroom.

What Works for Some Secondary Resource Room Teachers

1. Giving minicourses on study skills; test taking; orientation to junior high school; orientation to high school
2. Attending departmental meetings on a rotation basis: first week of the month, math; second week, english; third week, physical education, etc., until all departmental meetings have been attended
3. Participating in extracurricular activities to become aware of what is going on in a wide variety of classes
4. Becoming a faculty advisor to a club, sport, or activity
5. Developing a schoolwide peer tutoring program
6. Developing and teaching an in-service course on mainstreaming with a few content area teachers

BEHAVIORAL PROGRAMMING

In addition to developing, implementing, and monitoring the academic programs of students, the resource room teacher must also perform these functions for the behavioral program. Nationwide there are a wide variety of mildly disabled students attending the resource room (Friend and McNutt, 1984), and it is clear that their deficiencies are not limited to academic performances. Reynolds and Birch (1977) note that the inappropriate behaviors exhibited by special education students in the regular classroom present greater problems for the teacher than do the academic deficiencies. Clearly, this is not a textbook on classroom management, and those readers who lack such skills are directed to texts dealing with this topic. However, it is clear that resource room teachers can benefit from basic classroom management procedures. This section will focus on three sets of behaviors that need to be dealt with in the resource room: (1) minor disturbances, (2) moderate inappropriate behaviors, and (3) severe behavior problems.

Minor Disturbances

Minor disruptions do not have a terribly detrimental effect on the resource room program, but they still need to be dealt with in a consistent manner. One approach that has been effective in dealing with such problems has been dubbed "Super School." During the 1971-1972 and 1972-1973 academic years a demonstration classroom was established by the University of Kansas and the Lawrence (Kansas) Unified School District No. 497 for the purpose of applying behavioral management procedures in a regular classroom (Hopkins and Conard, 1976). The first year of the project focused on the third grade, and the second year focused on the third and fourth grades. The classes were heterogeneously grouped and included special education students who attended the resource room. some of the teaching methods employed were as follows:

1. *Praising students who were working.* The teacher verbally praised all students who were on task. Initially her rate was between five and ten per minute. Once appropriate behavior patterns were established, this practice was gradually faded.
2. *Descriptive praise.* A specific description of the behavior being reinforced helped the students understand why they were being reinforced, and it also served to cue other children. For example, "I like the way Mary is in her seat; she'll be able to complete her assignment."
3. *Praise across the room.* This procedure enabled the teacher to deliver reinforcement to a large number of students. Obviously she could not see their work, but she could reinforce appropriate on-task behavior.
4. *Nonverbal reinforcement.* In addition to verbal praise, many students respond to smiles, winks, pats on the back, hugs, and other types of nonverbal reinforcement. This approach also allows the teacher to deliver higher rates of approval.
5. *Privileges.* These were only given contingent upon appropriate behaviors. Too often students are given privileges for inappropriate behaviors, such as the student who is the monitor because he or she has engaged in inappropriate behavior and the teacher wants to "keep him or her busy." Inadvertently the teacher is reinforcing negative behaviors.
6. *Positive comments on papers.* All papers received some special comment regardless of the accuracy of the assignment. The teacher could comment on the effort expended, even if that effort did not produce the desirable results.

7. *Ignoring inappropriate behavior.* Because of the high rates of reinforcement, the teacher was able to ignore inappropriate behavior, and the greater majority of them were extinguished.
8. *A simple punishment procedure.* All classroom rules were clearly listed on the board. If a student broke these rules, a point was placed on the board. The student lost five minutes of recess time for each point. It is important to note that this approach was only used as a last resort. If a student received a large number of points, the teacher would check herself to see that she was reinforcing this student at appropriate levels.

The results of this project brought about a remarkable gain in academic and social behaviors. Often regular educators remark that the process of mainstreaming takes time away from nondisabled students. This project, as well as other research (Kazdin, 1973; Drabman and Lahey, 1974), indicates that there are vicarious effects of reinforcement. In "Super School," for example, the disabled students displayed marked improvement, but this improvement was even greater for their nondisabled peers. Clearly, the resource room teacher must be skilled in consultation with regular educators if a project such as "Super School" is to succeed.

The techniques employed in this project are fairly easy to implement in a resource room setting. Another set of procedures was recently discussed by McDaniel (1986). He notes that these procedures represent an eclectic point of view and have been demonstrated to be effective. They are as follows:

1. *The focusing principle.* Essentially, this basic principle suggests that the teacher should get the students' attention *prior to* giving instructions or presenting material. It lets the students know that the teacher believes that what he or she has to say is important.
2. *The principle of direct instruction.* This refers to getting students on task quickly and keeping them engaged in on-task behavior. Having a contract for the day or a file or folder that they can consult will alert them to their responsibilities and will prevent unnecessary interruptions.
3. *The monitoring principle.* Here McDaniel suggests frequent movement about the room to allow the teacher to evaluate student progress and performance. The teacher can provide feedback, prevent the student from "practicing failure," and refocus the student.

4. *The modeling principle.* Teachers must provide their students with good models of appropriate school behavior. Teachers should be prompt, organized, and well mannered and should exhibit self-control so that students will have a role model to emulate. At all costs, they should avoid sarcastic remarks and speak in a soft, low-pitched voice.
5. *The cuing principle.* McDaniels believes that good teachers have always used cues to improve discipline. A raised hand for silence, pointing to classroom rules, and employing a sign that says "work zone" can all help to remind students of the task at hand. The use of cues can be very helpful and allows the teacher to use his or her creativity in developing novel cues.
6. *The principles of environmental control.* One thing a teacher can exercise a great deal of control over is the classroom environment. A teacher can add or take away stimulating activities depending upon their effects on student behavior. This control can also be accomplished through teacher behavior, which can alternately stimulate or calm students in the class.
7. *The principle of low-profile intervention.* Management in the classroom should be as discreet, unobtrusive, and smooth as possible. Confrontations and public encounters should be avoided. Teachers must be aware of the need to anticipate behavioral difficulties and develop a systematic plan of interaction. This is much more effective than rapidly escalating a minor problem.
8. *The principle of assertive discipline.* This combination of reinforcement and limit setting has been set forth by Canter and calls for a higher-profile type of intervention. The assertive teacher clearly states the expectations for student behavior and develops positive and negative consequences for the class.
9. *The I- message principle.* Basically, I-messages can be employed in two ways: (1) by a specific request ("I want you to. . .") or (2) by communication of feelings ("when you do ______ I feel______ and it angers me"). McDaniels believes that both can be employed as one of the many interventions in a teacher's repertoire of effective classroom management techniques.
10. *The principle of positive reinforcement.* Perhaps the best-known method of classroom management, this essentially says "catch 'em when they're good." Teachers need to develop a wide variety of verbal and nonverbal reinforcement procedures, starting with praise and increasing in the reinforcement hierarchy to tangible rewards.

The above represent a basis for developing skills in classroom management and can eliminate most minor disturbances in a resource room.

Moderate Inappropriate Behaviors

There are behaviors that require a more consistent, data-based approach in order to be substantially reduced or eliminated. In these cases the resource room teacher must be skilled in identifying the behavior, in collecting and recording data, in using reinforcement techniques, and perhaps in using punishment techniques and a token economy system. Because of the small number of students attending the resource room, it is fairly easy to implement such a program.

Identifying Target Behaviors. The initial step in the development of a systematic intervention plan is the identification of a behavior in observable and measurable terms. Although this appears to be a reasonable and simple starting point, it often represents a major stumbling block for teachers, be they regular or special educators. It is common practice to assess academic problems through the use of objective instruments such as formal standardized tests, informal criterion-referenced tests, and teacher-made tests. We engage in such practices because it is crucial to pinpoint the students' strengths and weaknesses, how they approach tasks, and how they respond to instruction in order to develop a remedial program that has a high probability for success. However, we rarely apply such rigorous conditions to the assessment of behavioral problems. We often discuss a student's behavior in vague and nebulous terms or focus on the possible reasons for this behavior. Such discussions may be helpful in understanding the nature of a child's difficulty, but they will rarely, if ever, enable the resource room teacher to develop an intervention plan that can be carried out in the resource room or the regular classroom. A behavioral approach demands precision, from the identification of the behavior to the evaluation of the effectiveness of the intervention plan. Therefore, the teacher must define exactly what behaviors are to be increased or decreased: for example, whether he or she wants to increase in-seat behavior, to decrease the number of times Joseph talks out, to increase raising hands to ask a question, to decrease the number of times John hits Louis, and so forth. All of these behaviors can be observed: that is, we can see if the behavior occurs — we don't have to infer. Moreover, they can be measured: we can count the frequency or duration of each. Most, if not all, classroom behaviors can be stated in observable and measurable terms. Below is a list of behaviors typically emitted by special students in the mainstream. Column A presents the problem in nonbehavioral terms, and column B clearly defines the target behavior.

	A — Not Measurable		B — Measurable
1.	Student never pays attention.	1.	Increase the percentage of time the student spends on task (eye contact with the teacher, looking at textbook, writing when appropriate).
2.	Student is very hostile.	2.	Decrease the number of times the student hits another student.
3.	Student does not have any friends in the class.	3.	Increase the number of positive comments made to the target student by fellow classmates. Increase time spent with other students.
4.	Student has a poor self-concept.	4.	Increase the number of positive self-statements. Decrease negative comments regarding work or self.
5.	Student is always interrupting.	5.	Increase the number of times the student waits his or her turn to speak.
6.	Student wanders around the room.	6.	Increase in-seat behavior.
7.	Student is never on time.	7.	Increase on-time behavior during a specified period.
8.	Student does not respect others' property.	8.	Decrease the number of times the student defaces another student's work.
9.	Student appears to have a great deal on his or her mind.	9.	Decrease off-task behavior (looking out the window, lack of eye contact, not following directions).
10.	Student is a very aggressive child.	10.	Decrease the number of times the student pushes another student.

As can be seen from the above, refinement of the description of behaviors allows teachers to focus on a specific behavior, communicate more effectively with colleagues, administrators, and parents, and begin to collect data on the frequency and duration of behaviors emitted by those students who are in the resource room. The last mentioned, accurate recording keeping, is one of the cornerstones of a behavioral approach to classroom management. Often teachers believe that the paperwork associated with this approach is overwhelming. However, upon close examination they realize that it can be a very effective use of time. Madsen and Madsen (1974) discuss a case in which a teacher refused to "waste [her] time with all that book work" (p. 31). When observed by an independent observer, this teacher was recorded saying "now stop that talking" 143 times in one morning session. Obviously these negative comments took considerable time away from teaching, whereas the record-keeping procedures could be developed so that they would be less time-consuming and more productive than the repetition of negative instructions.

There are numerous recording methods available to the behavioral scientist (Kalish, 1981), but four appear to have the greatest applicability for the special education resource room teacher. They are (1) event recording, (2) duration recording, (3) time sample recording, and (4) direct measurement of permanent products.

Event Recording. This involves the collection of raw frequencies of behavior. It is used for discrete events, those typically lasting less than two minutes. Behaviors that lend themselves to this type of recording are the number of times a child is out of his or her seat, the number of times a student comes late to class, the number of times a student talks out in the classroom, and the number of times a student hits his or her classmates. Holms (1966) employed this type of recording to count the disruptive classroom behaviors of a nine-year-old boy. Physical aggression was the target behavior of a study undertaken by Brown and Elliott (1965) which also employed this method of collecting data.

Clearly, the teacher must be able to collect the data in a manner that does not interfere with the ability of the teacher to move about the room and provide instruction to students. The author has found a wrist golf counter the best device for this purpose (see *Journal of Applied Behavioral Analysis* (1968) *1*, 77-78). It allows the teacher movement and provides him or her with a readily available, inconspicuous data collection device. Other ways in which events can be recorded are by marking a piece of adhesive tape adhered to the wrist, moving small objects (paper, tokens, toothpicks, etc.) from one pocket to another, or using a small tally sheet or index card. Usually a thirty-minute observation period is adequate.

Duration Recording. When behaviors occur for a long period of time, duration recording is the most appropriate procedure. Certain behaviors, such as temper tantrums, leaving the classroom, and taking time off task, may not occur frequently but may occur for a relatively long period of time. When a behavior occurs for longer than two or three minutes, collecting data on the time elapsed may be more meaningful than recording the actual frequency of the event. A number of researchers employed this recording procedure in their investigations. Madsen and Madsen (1974) recorded the percentage of time a seven-year-old girl was sucking her thumb, and the percentage of time spent on task was recorded by Ferritor, et al. (1972). Although a stop watch would be the most accurate way to collect this data, the minute hand on a wall clock or wrist watch can be used as long as the recorder can keep an accurate record of the time elapsed. The obervation period will be dependent upon the type of target behaviors.

Time Sample Recording. Some behaviors occur so frequently that it is virtually impossible to count every event; in these cases a sampling procedure is followed. In time sampling, an observation period is divided into equal intervals. If a student emits the target behavior at the end of the specified interval, it is recorded as a plus; if he or she does not emit the behavior, it is recorded as a minus. In the illustration below, a thirty-minute period is divided into 10 three-minute intervals in order to record the percentage of time a student is in his or her seat. Through the use of a stop watch, wall clock, or wrist watch, the teacher observes the student at each three-minute segment. At the three-minute interval the student was in the seat; therefore a plus was recorded. At the six-minute interval the student was out of the seat; therefore a minus was recorded. This process is continued until the thirty-minute period expires. The percentage of time spent in seat is obtained by dividing the number of intervals into the number of intervals of in-seat behavior and converting this figure to a percentage. In this case the student was in his or her seat 50 percent of the time.

In-Seat Behavior (30-minute intervals)

+	-	+	-	+	+	+	-	-	-
3	6	9	12	15	18	21	24	27	30

Although a thirty-minute interval is used most often, longer observation intervals may be necessary for specific types of behaviors.

Direct Measurement of Permanent Products. Although inappropriate behaviors are problems unto themselves, often they interfere with the acquisition of academic skills. To obtain data on this interference, the teacher can record data on a number of items, such as teacher-made tests, workbooks, pages completed, and the like. These data can be presented in raw frequency or percentages. Madsen and Forsythe (1974) used direct measurement of a permanent product to record the accuracy of the responses of sixth-grade students when they worked with an individual mathematics kit. In such cases teachers merely record the students' score on a daily basis. The tendency is to use this data collection procedure exclusively for academic tasks, but its utility in recording the occurrence of academic behaviors that are caused by behavioral problems (such as off-task behavior) should not be overlooked.

Charting Baseline Data. All behavioral data can be displayed in a similar fashion on a graph. The ordinate (vertical axis) is labeled with a scale representing the behaviors emitted in terms of frequency or percentage, and the abscissa (horizontal axis) is labeled with the time dimensions, such as minutes, days, or observations (Hall, 1971). Teachers will want to collect and display data in such a way so that they will be able to evaluate the effectiveness of their intervention plan. Typically baseline data are collected for a least one week; then an intervention plan is implemented. A more detailed explanation of each of these stages follows.

If we are to make educational decisions based on factual information, not intuition or feelings, then we must add precision to our teaching. The first step is to establish the *baseline,* which can be defined as the operant level of behavior (Hall, 1971), that is, the level of behavior prior to intervention. Therefore, during the first five days of data collection, the student must be unaware of the procedure so that an accurate reading can be obtained. Typically, the baseline will last five days, but one must examine the data prior to moving on to the next stage. In baseline A in figure 6, a desirable behavior, such as in-seat behavior, is increasing; therefore, one should simply continue taking baseline data. In baseline B, an undesirable behavior, such as yelling out, is decreasing by itself; therefore, one should not implement an intervention but should continue to observe the behavior and record baseline data. A stable baseline is illustrated in baseline C. It is going up and down but is within reasonable parameters; therefore, it is appropriate to intervene.

Next a plan must be developed and implemented which will either increase an appropriate behavior or decrease an inappropriate one. An example is presented on the following pages. The behavior is to increase

Figure 6

Three Types of Baselines

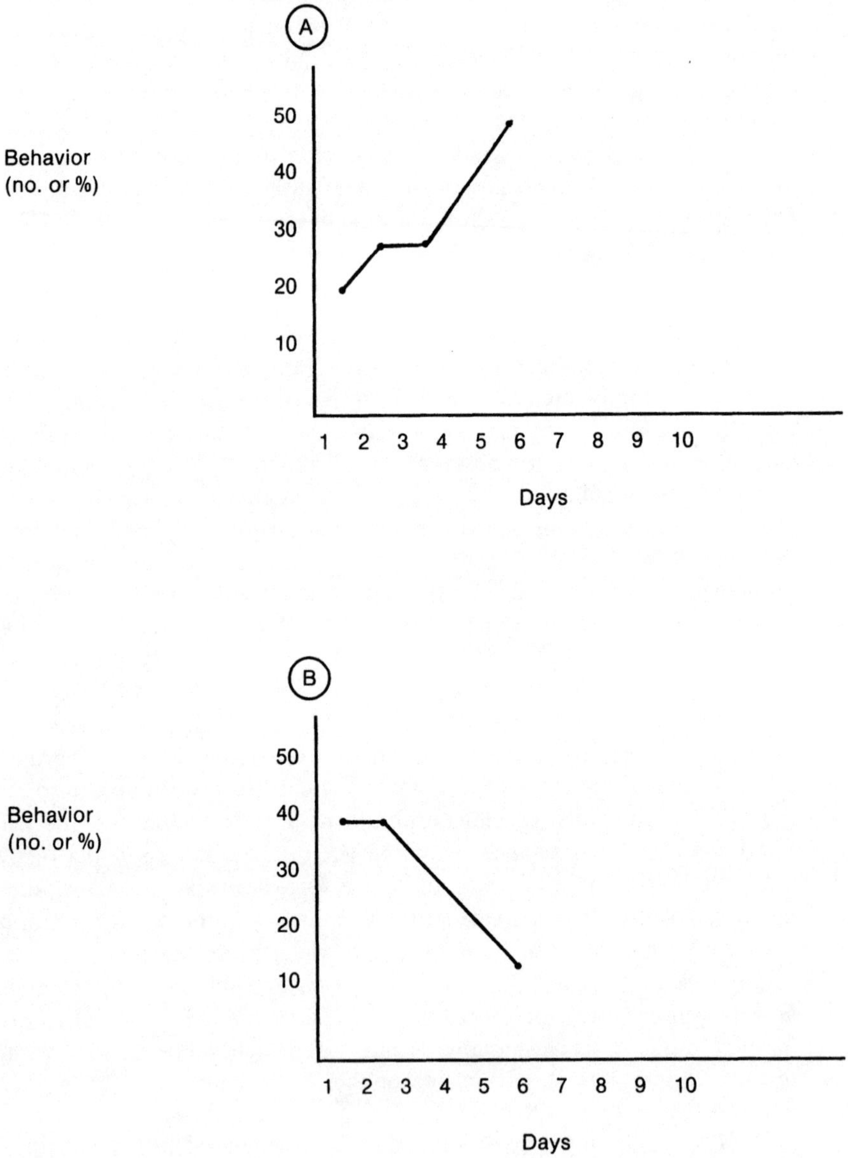

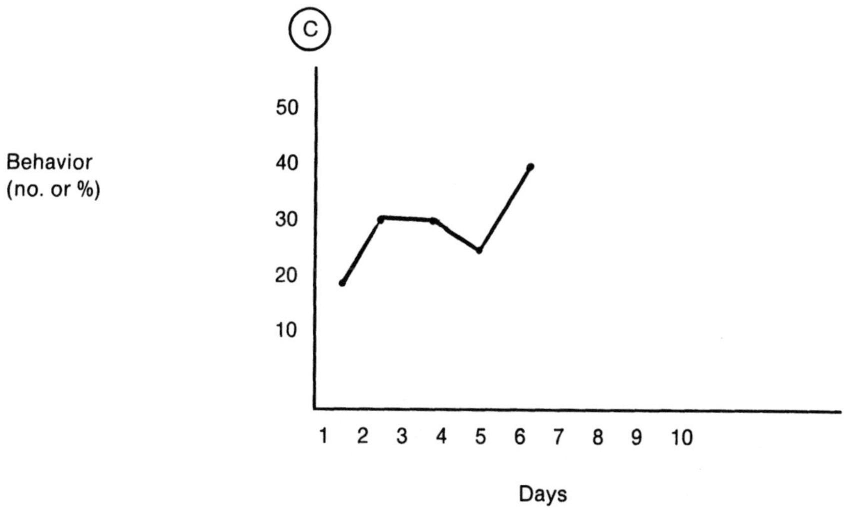

as a result of the intervention. The stable baseline enables the observer to begin the intervention on day 6 (see figure 7). The importance of charting behavior cannot be overemphasized. It is imperative if we are to add precision to our teaching in the special education or mainstreamed setting.

Reinforcement. "Any stimulus which regularly and reliably elicits a response" is a reinforcer (Kalish, 1981, p. 122). The contingent use of reinforcement, that is applying reinforcement after an appropriate behavior has been emitted, has brought about an increase in a wide variety of behaviors emitted by children and adolescents in educational settings. Hall et al. (1971) used contingent teacher attention and praise to decrease "talking out" in a special class setting. There has been consistent evidence that teacher attention (teacher proximity, verbal and nonverbal approvals) may act as an effective reinforcer for perschool and school-age children (Harris et al., 1966; Hawkins et. al., 1966; Thomas, Becker, and Armstrong, 1968; Shutte and Hopkins, 1970; Parsonson, Baer, and Baer, 1974; Madsen and Madsen, 1981). Bushell (1973) notes that "it has already been established that approval and praise of the teacher is an effective reinforcer for most children" (p. 71). Teacher approval is perhaps the most easily accessible technique of reinforcement and should be used in resource room and regular classroom settings to increase appropriate student behavior. Madsen and Madsen (1981) report that teachers who engage in high approval rates

Figure 7

Sample Graph Showing Baseline and Intervention Data

Student's name

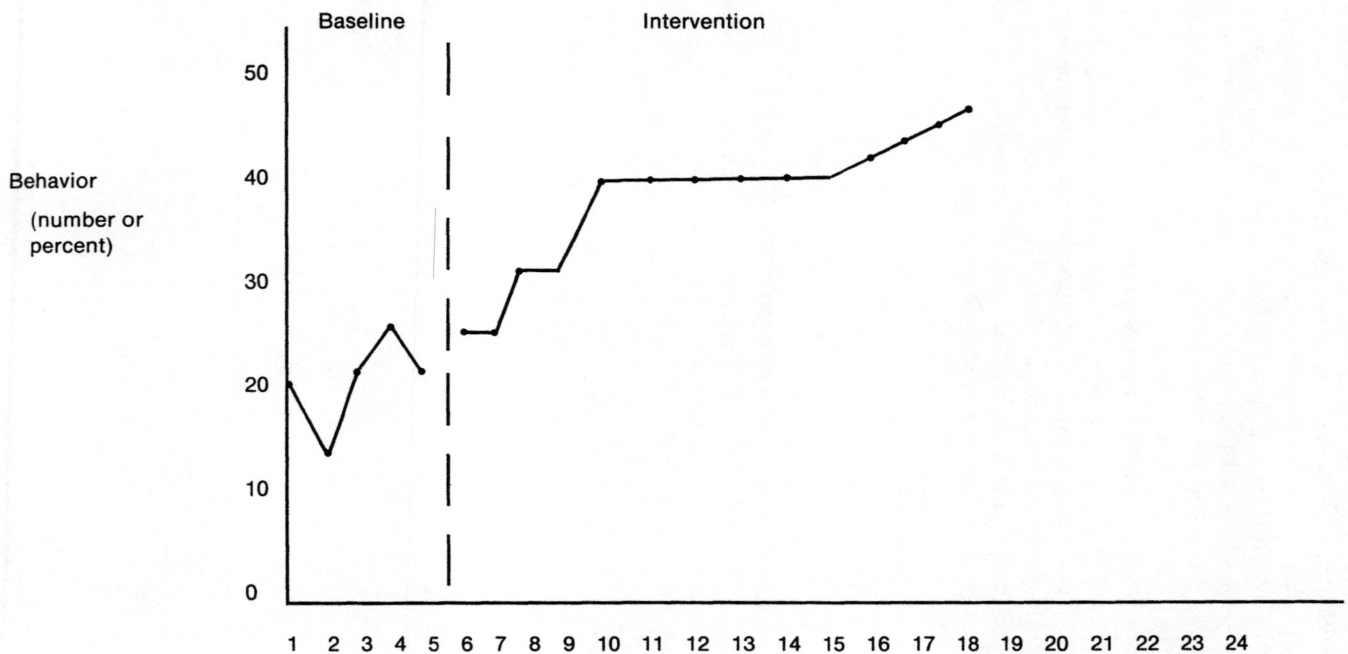

have less behavior problems in the classroom. They conclude that this improvement in behavior is directly related to the amount of attention teachers give to appropriate student behavior. Therefore, reinforcing appropriate behavior and (to a great extent) ignoring inappropriate behaviors should be a management tool used by all teachers. Other reinforcers that can be employed in the mainstreamed setting are free time, privileges, stars, stickers, notes, positive notes to parents, and the like. For a thorough list of reinforcers available in most classrooms, see Madsen and Madsen (1981), pp. 182-192.

Punishment. A punishment is anything that decreases the strength of a behavior (Hall, 1971). It is imperative that resource room teachers be aware of the negative effects of punishment. O'Leary and O'Leary (1976) caution teachers to use this technique sparingly because students tend to associate the punisher with the punishment. This relationship will clearly interfere with the establishment of a good rapport between teacher and student. Hall (1971) has also noted that one does not build up a repertoire of appropriate behaviors by employing punishment techniques; one simply eliminates the inappropriate behavior. Also to be considered is the effect of modeling this behavior for students who view the teacher as a standard for appropriate behavior. In most cases behaviors can be changed through the systematic application of reinforcement techniques. However, there may be times when a negative consequence is necessary to change a behavior. Tate and Baroff (1966), Bucher and King (1971), Koegal and Covert (1972), Hanser (1973), and O'Leary and O'Leary (1976) have used punishment techniques ranging from verbal reprimands to removal of privileges to reduce inappropriate student behaviors. Greer and Dorow (1976) note that punishment is not the first choice and that an approval rate of four to one is most desirable: that is, the teacher should be emitting at least four positive commands for every one negative comment. Investigations by Madsen and Madsen (1974), White (1975), and McNamara (1977) indicate that this is not the prevailing mode of teacher behavior.

Token Economies. Token economies have been employed in various environments, including the classroom (Kazdin, 1982). Briefly, such a system involves having students earn tokens (or points, stars, checks, etc.) contingent upon desired behaviors. At a later time, usually the end of the week, the student can exchange his or her tokens for prizes. These prizes may be edibles, toys, privileges in the classroom, or virtually anything available that can serve as a reinforcer. As Stephens and Cooper (1980) point out, tokens are not a cure-all, nor are they ends in themselves. Hall (1971) notes that they should only be employed as a last resort, when other reinforcers fail to bring about desired changes in behavior. Teachers must also realize that the record keeping involved with tokens is extensive and may not be a cost effective use of time. Other disadvantages, as well as advantages, of the token economy are listed by Stephens and Cooper (1980).

Contracting. If resource room students are to succeed, there must be improved communication between regular and special educators regarding the students' homework contracts reinforce appropriate behavior and improve academic and social behaviors. Homme (1970) describes the many uses of contracts in the classroom. They can be used for special subjects, academic subjects, homework assignments, or other similar areas of schoolwork that need specific attention. An example of a homework contract is presented in figure 8. The teacher and student jointly decide on the number of assignments that must be completed as to the reward that will be given.

Structured Learning. Goldstein, et al. (1980) have developed a program to teach adolescents appropriate prosocial behaviors. They employ a structured learning approach that incorporates examples of competent skill behavior, opportunities to rehearse, systematic feedback, and transfer of skill to real-life settings. They have identified fifty structured learning skills, which are presented below. Resource room teachers can select those skills that are appropriate for their students with moderate inappropriate behaviors and can follow the specific guidelines described by Goldstein and his colleagues (1980, pp. 84, 85).

Group I. — Beginning Social Skills

1. Listening
2. Starting a Conversation
3. Having a Conversation
4. Asking a Question
5. Saying Thank You
6. Introducing Yourself
7. Introducing Other People
8. Giving a Compliment

Group II — Advanced Social Skills

9. Asking for Help
10. Joining In
11. Giving Instructions
12. Following Instructions
13. Apologizing
14. Convincing Others

Group III — Skills for Dealing with Feelings

15. Knowing Your Feelings
16. Expressing Your Feelings
17. Understanding the Feelings of Others
18. Dealing with Someone Else's Anger
19. Expressing Affection
20. Dealing with Fear
21. Rewarding Yourself

Group IV — Skill Alternatives to Aggression

22. Asking Permission
23. Sharing Something
24. Helping Others
25. Negotiating
26. Using Self-control
27. Standing Up for Your Rights
28. Responding to Teasing
29. Avoiding Trouble with Others
30. Keeping Out of Fights

Group V — Skills for Dealing with Stress

31. Making a Complaint
32. Answering a Complaint
33. Showing Sportsmanship after the Game
34. Dealing with Embarrassment
35. Dealing with Being Left Out
36. Standing Up for a Friend
37. Responding to Persuasion
38. Responding to Failure
39. Dealing with Contradictory Messages
40. Dealing with an Accusation
41. Getting Ready for a Difficult Conversation
42. Dealing with Group Pressure

Group VI — Planning Skills

43. Deciding on Something to Do
44. Deciding What Caused a Problem
45. Setting a Goal
46. Deciding on Your Abilities
47. Gathering Information
48. Arranging Problems by Importance
49. Making a Decision
50. Concentrating on a Task

Severe Behavior Problems

There are students who attend the resource room who consistently display severely inappropriate behaviors and who appear to lack an understanding of appropriate rules of conducting oneself in school. For these students it may be necessary to teach social skills directly. Initially, the teacher must assess those skills that need to be taught. Typically these social skills can be identified in terms of problem behaviors. Cartledge and Milburn (1980) list the following problem behaviors and accompanying social skills to be taught (pp. 24, 25):

Problem Behaviors	*Social Skills*
1. The child calls others by uncomplimentary names.	1. The child makes positive remarks to others.
2. The child frequently interrupts the conversation of others.	2. The child waits for pauses in the conversation before speaking.
3. The child makes negative statements about his or her ability.	3. The child identifies something he or she does well.
4. The child cheats when playing games with peers.	4. The child plays games according to the rules.
5. The child has tantrums when teased by peers.	5. The child responds to peer teasing by ignoring or some other appropriate response.
6. The child laughs at or ignores individuals in need of help.	6. The child assists individuals in need of help.

Figure 8

Sample Homework Contract

STUDENT'S NAME ______________________

HOMEWORK

SUBJECT	MON.	TUES.	WED.	THURS.	FRI.
READING					
MATH					
SPELLING					
HAND WRITING					

I will complete ______________________ homework assignments.

My reward will be ______________________

Teacher ______________________ Date ______________________
(signature)

Student ______________________ Renegotiated on ______________________
(signature)

The resource room teacher may identify target social skills for individual students, as well as for groups. If possible, these skills should be taught in groups. Silverman, Zigmond, and Sansone (1981) suggest that one resource room period per week be reserved for group instruction in social skills. The teaching process can be broken into five steps: (1) providing instructions, (2) exposure to a model, (3) rehearsal, (4) performance feedback, and (5) practice (Cartledge and Milburn, 1980).

Providing Instructions. Students with learning or behavioral problems frequently require direct instruction for those skills that able learners appear to acquire incidentally. Most certainly this is the case with social skills. The special education resource room teacher must provide explicit instructions about the skill to be taught. This can be done through the use of specific objectives from the student's IEP or by generating lists of expected bheaviors for a wide variety of social skills. For example, Silverman, Zigmond, and Sanzone (1981) have identified a group of skills subsumed under the head *teacher pleasing behaviors.* Anyone who has worked in a special education setting is well aware of the problems the students have when interacting with regular classroom teachers. It is often observed that these students do not know how to "get along" with these teachers. Using the five-stage process developed by Cartledge and Milburn (1980) and the content from the teacher pleasing behavior part of the School Survival Skills Program (Silverman, Zigmond and Sanzone, 1981), the resource room teacher would begin by providing instructions. For example, students must realize that certain behaviors are expected in each classroom. At times these rules will be explicit, and at other times they must be inferred. Perhaps the simplest approach would be to briefly discuss what is expected in general, such as by saying "All students are expected to be in class on time," or "All students must bring a pen and paper to class" or "All students are expected to raise their hand before talking." The teacher must provide the students with sufficient information to enable them to understand what is expected of them. Often students act in an inappropriate fashion because it was assumed that they knew how to behave. This approach makes no such assumption; it provides the resource room student with the instructions necessary to comprehend what the expected behavior is prior to engaging in a violation of a social skill.

Exposure to a Model. Instructions alone will be insufficient to bring about an increase in social skills. Students must have an opportunity to observe individuals that model the appropriate behavior. This can be done in a number of ways through the use of role playing, pictorial representations, films, slides, books, and the like. Ample exposure to appropriate models will enable students to see how the social skill can be manifested in a wide variety of settings and under different conditions.

Rehearsals. "Trying out" correct behavior in the secure setting of the resource room is the next step in the process. Students should be encouraged to think about the setting in which the social skill is to be demonstrated and to practice the skill. Some students find the use of visual imagery very helpful. They try to imagine the situation in the regular classroom and "see" themselves carrying out the appropriate social skill successfully. Role playing is also helpful when rehearsing a social skill. Students can try out the social skill as other students play the role of the teacher and other students.

Performance Feedback. During the rehearsal of social skills the resource room teacher must evaluate the student's performance. Although these activities are enjoyable in and of themselves, the goal is to increase the students' ability to increase their social skills. Therefore, feedback must be given to enable them to refine their understanding of the procedure. The feedback should be immediate and overwhelmingly positive: that is, the same principles of reinforcement discussed previously apply here. Students should be provided with frequent positive feedback regarding their preformance. At times, neutral comments may need to be made about a specific skill, but all efforts must be made to ensure that students do not receive punitive rewards regarding their ability to rehearse the social skill.

Practice. Once the social skill has been demonstrated in the resource room, the student is ready to generalize the skill to the regular classroom. It is obvious that this is the goal of social skill training; it is not sufficient to display these behaviors in the resource room alone. Ample opportunity must be given for practicing the skill in the regular classroom, and reinforcement must be given contingent upon emitting the skill in that setting.

4

Communicating with Educators and Parents

WHY CONSULT?

Periodically, there is a hue and cry from the teaching profession when legislators, administrators, or the general public attempt to hold teachers responsible for the improvement made by their students. If this demand causes considerable concern for the teacher in a regular classroom, imagine the situation of the resource room teacher. To a large extent the success or failure of the resource room program is dependent upon the teacher's ability to have the appropriate modifications and programs carried out in the regular classroom setting. Most likely students will attend the resource room for one or two hours per day, five days per week. Even if they attend for a larger period of time, the placement is still considered "part-time" (Thurlow et al., 1983). For the remainder of the school day these students are in the regular classroom with a teacher (or teachers) who may have very little information regarding special education in general and the nature and needs of a student attending the resource room in particular.

Therefore, it is not surprising that the early resource room models provided specific guidelines for consulting with regular education colleagues. Reger (1969) states that programs should allocate at least 15 percent of the resource room teacher's time for working with regular educators. Cienion (1968) proposes one hour per day and one-half day on Friday in order to accomplish this task. And although others have not made specific suggestions regarding the allocation of time, all have noted the importance of this component of the resource room teacher's role. This may be the most critical aspect of that role. All the diagnostic and programming information available will be of little use if the student does not have the opportunity to transfer skills acquired in the resource room to the regular education setting. The regular classroom teacher must be provided with adequate information and resources if the student is to succeed, and the resource room teacher must learn how the regular education classroom is organized and have knowledge of the classroom curriculum. The answer to the question "Why should I consult with the regular classroom teacher?" is quite simple: without consultation most, if not all, of the efforts expended in the confines of the resource room will be for naught.

WHAT "THEY" WANT TO KNOW

Although the notion of communicating with regular education colleagues seems somewhat easy to apply, it is not. Indeed, Cohen and Safran (1981) report that first-year resource room teachers rated working cooperatively with regular educators as their most significant problem. Deno and Merkin (1977) report that many of the resource room teachers that they have worked with preferred spending all their time with students — not colleagues. Speece and Mandell (1980) offer additional insight into this problem when they report that regular educators are not particularly satisfied with the amount of communication they have had with resource room teachers. In the implementation of workshops for regular educators dealing with special education students the author has also found that there is a great deal of dissatisfaction on the part of regular educators regarding their resource room teacher colleagues.

It appears that a reasonable first step in attempting to resolve this problem is to provide regular classroom teachers with information that they will find useful. As previously noted, an informal survey was administered to regular educators in order to gather this information (McNamara, 1981). What emerged were requests for very specific information. It appears that the regular educator desires a great deal of information that may appear impossible to provide short of developing an in-service course (which may be a useful course of action). However, what is important to recognize is that the concerns evidenced by one's colleagues are legitimate. The experience of the author suggests that the first step in the process of effective communication is the awareness of the need to engage in this activity. Resource room teachers who are successful in this role must first understand the importance of providing this information and must then develop strategies for doing so. This is even more important given the recent remarks by Will (1986) and Reynolds, Wang, and Walberg (1987) regarding the need for universal cooperation and communication between special and regular education. What follows are some of those strategies.

STRATEGIES FOR COMMUNICATING WITH REGULAR EDUCATORS

Initially resource room teachers must find out what the needs of the staff are in their particular building. This can be accomplished through the use of a simple needs assessment to be distributed to the staff during the first week of school. It can be open-ended (see figure 9) or more directed (see figure 10). This assessment gives the regular classroom teacher an opportunity to provide significant input and at the same time demonstrates an awareness, on the part of the resource room teacher, of the importance of cooperative planning.

Concurrently the resource room teacher should be developing a booklet (see figure 11) to be presented to the staff during the first few weeks of the school year. Although the format will vary, the content should include, at the very least, the overall philosophy of the resource room, the teacher's schedule, services that can be provided, testing modifications, and resources available for teacher use. This approach prevents confusion as to "what goes on down there" in the resource room. Frequently, regular educators are kept in the dark about the resource room. It is the job of the resource room teacher to shed some light on the program and to develop good public relations skills. A booklet of this type should be written in jargon-free language that can clearly communicate with teachers not trained in special education.

The above remarks are general in nature. Classroom teachers also need specific information regarding their students who attend the resource room. A general description of the student, his or her learning problems, or a classification is simply insufficient. What is called for is a profile that clearly states each student's strengths, weaknesses, and any other information that will assist the teacher. Figure 12 is an example of such a profile. After considerable revisions, resource room teachers in one school district have found this to be a useful device (Bornstein and Lauber, 1986).

Figure 9

Needs Assessment Letter (Open-Ended)

Dear ______________________________________,

As you know, there are students in your class who attend the same resource room (see attached list). If you have any questions and concerns regarding these student(s), please jot them down on the space provided below and drop this sheet in my mailbox. I will also be sending you a booklet within the next few weeks that will describe my program more fully. Please feel free to drop by my room anytime. I'm in Room 117.

Sincerely,

Figure 10

Needs Assessment Letter (Structured)

Dear ______________________________________,

As you know, there are students in your class who attend the same resource room (see attached list). So that I can provide you with information about these students, I'd appreciate it if you'd take a few minutes to check those items listed below that you would like to discuss:

________ Nature of the disability

________ Goals of the resource room

________ Approximate methods and materials

________ Grading

________ Parent meetings

________ Scheduling

________ The Individual Educational Plan (IEP)

Within two weeks I will be sending you a booklet that will provide you with information on my program. In the meantime, always feel free to stop by. I'm in room 117.

Sincerely,

Figure 11

Resource Room Booklet: Sample Table of Contents

Figure 12

Sample Student Profile (Harborfields Central School District, Oldfield Middle School, Greenlawn, New York; from Bornstein and Lauber, 1986).

Resource Room

To:

From:

Date:

The following checklist has been compiled to acquaint you with ____________ strengths, weaknesses, and compensatory needs. This assessment is based on historical data available at the present time.

Strengths	Weaknesses	Motor Activity
____	____	Handwriting
____	____	speed
____	____	accuracy
____	____	letter formation (size, spacing, reversal, slant, addition, omission, legibility)
____	____	Cutting with scissor
____	____	Drawing or tracing
____	____	Sewing or knitting
____	____	Building or creating craft objects
____	____	Balance
____	____	Rhythm
____	____	Directionality (ability to know right from left, up from down)

		Perceptual
____	____	Visual
____	____	memory
____	____	sequencing
____	____	interpreting material (newspaper, photographs — detail, facts, etc.)
____	____	attention to visual material
____	____	organization
____	____	visual-motor (copying from blackboard)
____	____	Auditory
____	____	retention of data presented orally
____	____	listening to lecture
____	____	discrimination (ability to hear similarities and differences between two or more sounds).
____	____	Social perception
____	____	gets along with peers
____	____	says appropriate things to others
		Spoken Language
____	____	Understanding multiple meanings
____	____	Eliciting words for common objects
____	____	Making needs known
____	____	Following simple routine instructions
____	____	Relating a story or experience in a logical and sequential fashion
____	____	Formulating words and sentences
		Written Language
____	____	Spelling
____	____	Expressing and organizing thoughts (categorizing and sequencing)
____	____	Syntax and grammar
____	____	Vocabularly
____	____	Mechanics (punctuation, capitalization, etc.)

		Arithmetic
____	____	Quantitative language (more, less, before, after)
____	____	Word problems
____	____	Time telling
____	____	Measurement
____	____	Monetary values
____	____	Computational skills
		Compensatory Needs
____	____	Needs to take tests in resource room
____	____	Calculator
____	____	Dictation
____	____	Reader
____	____	Extended time for criterion-referenced competency, and classroom testing

Reading Level		**Math Level**
________	Average for grade	________
________	Below average	________
________	Above average	________

Behavior:

____

____

____

____

Additional Comments:

____

____

____

____

____

It may well appear that the position of resource room teacher is best filled by an individual with a degree in public relations, not special education. To be sure, a resource room teacher is indeed attempting to build good public relations for the program and its students. However, the underlying rationale is that such a relationship will increase the probability of success for the students. Resource room teachers must be aware of the importance of input from regular educators and the need to develop a relationship based on mutual trust. Regularly scheduled meetings should be scheduled in order to move in this direction. From time to time the resource room teacher should drop a note in the regular teacher's mailbox to inquire about students (see Figure 13), and if NCR (no carbon required) paper is used, the teacher will always have a record of his or her contacts. Figure 14 illustrates a form that requires little writing and that may be enlarged for those colleagues who find the former note too lengthy.

Below are a number of other ways in which special education resource room teachers have developed good relations with their regular education colleagues. Although all may not be possible in every setting, they represent efforts worthy of consideration.

— Have coffee and cake available every Friday morning before school starts for those teachers with students who attend the resource room.
— Schedule periodic working lunches to go over specific concerns of teachers.
— Find out where teachers congregate — teachers' lounge, offices, lunchroom, — and casually drop in.
— Be sure to eat lunch where most teachers eat. Don't be an isolate.
— Keep a log of your contacts with teachers and evaluate it periodically. You may realize that you are missing some people over time.
— Park your car near a teacher you want to speak with and strike up a conversation before or after school.
— Start an after-school jogging club or exercise club or the like to get to know as many teachers as possible.
— Actively participate in schoolwide events — dances, sporting events, plays, musicals, — to become better known and to demonstrate concern for the school in general.
— Become an advisor for a club or a coach for a team.

As with all interpersonal contacts, one has to be careful not to overstep one's boundaries. Some of the activities listed above may appear to be too pushy, too aggressive, too assertive. This can be a problem. The resource room teacher must be aggressive and assertive, but can

Figure 13

Inquiry Note to Classroom Teacher (Harborfields Central School District, Oldfield Middle School, Greenlawn, New York; from Bornstein and Lauber, 1986).

Resource Room

Student Inquiry

To: ______________________

From: ______________________

Date: ______________________

This information is for the period ______________ to ______________.

How is ______________________ doing in your class?

Work due? ______________________

____

____

Recent test grades? ______________________

____

____

Attendance and lateness? ______________________

____

____

Other Comments ______________________

____

____

Thank you.

Figure 14

Simple Inquiry Note

To: ____________________

From: ____________________

Date: ____________________

Please check the appropriate items below for ____________________.

____ Assignments are handed in on time.

____ Assignments are handed in late.

____ Assignments have not been completed.

____ Test scores are satisfactory.

____ Test scores are unsatisfactory.

____ Attends class regularly.

____ Misses class frequently.

____ Is always on time.

____ Is frequently late.

____ Is on task during class.

____ Is off task during class.

____ We need to speak.

____ It is not necessary to speak at this time.

Additional comments: ____________________

____

____

Thank you.

do so in such a manner as to not offend other colleagues. Those individuals who heed the advice of Deno and Merkin (1977) will more than likely be able to actively involve regular classroom teachers in the resource room program and will do so in a nonthreatening, respectful manner. Below are some dos and don'ts for consultants (adpated from material developed by Diagnostic Prescriptive Teachers, Minneapolis Public Schools).

DO

remember that people *are* capable of solving their own problems.

try to accept others' values.

be fully aware of your own values.

have a specific way that teachers can get your help.

be knowledgeable about all school and community resources available.

to save time and help more teachers, learn how to use your services; meet with a teaching team or department at meeting times.

have a wide variety of materials to help teachers.

let teachers know you value their knowledge.

try to be involved in school activities.

DON'T

tell a teacher you will help with a child without spelling out exactly what you think your responsibilities are.

schedule yourself so tightly that you don't have time to meet with teachers for immediate consultation.

act as if you have all the answers to solve a teacher's problem.

become the "middle man" to take a teacher's gripes to the principal.

push when the consultee is not ready to move.

let your need to help get in the way of the needs of the consultee.

expect to see immediate results — you'll get discouraged.

One way to make sure to touch base with all of the teachers of the resource room students is to keep a simple file. A loose-leaf binder divided according to grade (elementary level) or content area (secondary level) will be sufficient. The resource room teacher simply records each teacher's schedule and the resource room students in that class. Every time a contact is made, he or she writes down the date, what was discussed, and any resolution. At the beginning of each section should be listed all the teachers for that grade or content area, and every other week the dates should be transferred to this master list. In this way the resource room teacher can quickly see whether he or she has missed any teachers or has met with some much more than others. Any other useful information should also be included, such as the parking lot the classroom teacher uses, the time the teacher arrives at school, where the teacher eats lunch (and if he or she does not want to be bothered at this time), and when the teacher leaves for home.

WORKING WITH PARENTS

This information will enable the resource room teacher to have frequent, sporadic, and "spontaneous" meetings that will lead to a more substantive formal discussion of the student in question. This record-keeping procedure has been employed by many successful resource room teachers. Although it takes a little extra time to set up, it is fairly easy to maintain.

Kroth (1985) has formulated a hypothesis regarding the interaction between home and school. He states that "cooperative home-school programs will accelerate pupils' academic behaviors and decrease undesirable social behaviors" (p. 41). It appears that this is a reasonable hypothesis for all educators, in particular those working in special education resource rooms. Frequently, resource room teachers serve as the liaison between the school and the home. Therefore, they must possess those competencies that allow them to carry out this difficult task with skill. Furthermore, as special educators, they are responsible for Individual Education Program (IEP) meetings, in addition to traditional parent-teacher conferences. This section will discuss these and other issues that pertain to the development and implementation of an effective communication system between school and home.

General Guidelines

The field of special education is replete with technical jargon. Too often special education teachers employ these terms when discussing a student's difficulty during a meeting with parents. Rather than getting their point across to parents, this approach simply sets up a barrier to communication (McNamara, 1979). It is imperative that special education resource room teachers use jargon-free language when talking with parents. This is not to suggest a lack of sophistication or knowledge on the part of the parent. Jargon is simply ineffective because the listener may not understand what one is saying, and so the purpose of the meeting is lost. It is far better to attempt to describe terms in such a way that the parent will have examples of the specific behaviors and tasks in which their child is engaging. Parents must feel that the teacher has their best interest in mind. The manner in which one builds this type of trusting relationship will depend on one's particular style. However, there are a number of strategies to consider. Margolis and Brannigan (1986, pp. 72, 73) list eight of them:

1. *Accept parents as they are and do not try to induce fundamental changes.* Trying to change parents in some basic way communicates that something is wrong with them. For example, it would be a mistake to attempt to convince parents who are ardent supporters of the "back-to-basics movement" that a values clarification curriculum is more important to children. In conflict situations especially, the less one tries to change broad-based, philosophical beliefs of people, the greater one's ultimate chance of influencing them. At a later point in time, when trust is high, parents may demonstrate their readiness to change by asking for assistance in learning new concepts or skills.
2. *Listen carefully and empathetically for the cognitive and emotional content of the parents' message.* Teachers must give their complete, undivided, uninterrupted attention and must communicate that they understand during natural pauses. Statements should be short and to the point, using fresh words to summarize the parents' thoughts and feelings.
3. *Help parents feel comfortable and share information and resources with them when legally permissible.* Small talk about mutual interests or experiences unrelated to the issues of contention and a symbolic "cup of coffee" frequently help parents feel more comfortable. Providing help and requesting legitimate assistance from parents establishes natural trust-building opportunities. Sharing information, resources, and ideas is a powerful process in building trust. On the other hand, evading requests for information or obscuring pertinent facts immediately creates the impression that one is hiding something important and heightens distrust and defensiveness.
4. *Prepare for meetings by studying pertinent materials beforehand so that a high level of knowledge will be apparent at the right moment.* Parents need to trust not only the teacher's objectives but also his or her knowledge and professional competency. It is critical that the teacher shares relevant information at natural opportunities without lecturing, dominating, or conveying the slightest attitude of superiority. A few well-choosen comments or questions, devoid of technical information or relevant details, will create doubts about one's competency and interest.
5. *Focus on the parents' hopes, aspirations, concerns, and needs.* Parents' negative feelings toward school personnel usually arise from fear that their child's welfare is being jeopardized. Unilaterally setting agendas for parents, rather than focusing on their concerns, only intensifies distrust and resistance. It is natural to like someone who is interested in one's concerns. Attending to parents' concerns communicates caring.

6. *Keep one's word.* This is a simple rule, but is sadly often forgotten. If one promises a return telephone call by two o'clock, one should make it on time. Making the call promptly communicates respect and reliability.
7. *Allow parents' expertise to shine.* Parents are knowledgeable about many aspects of their child's development. Asking for their opinions, inviting them to comment on whether or not the student's behavior in school is representative of his or her behavior at home, and asking if one's viewpoints or suggestions appear to make sense to them (for example, "I was wondering if you have any thoughts about what I just said. If so, I'd appreciate your sharing them with me") facilitate trust and help establish the teacher as someone who values them. Providing knowledgeable answers in response to questions is desirable if it does not take the form of pontification, intimidation (for example, through the use of jargon, such as "perceptual problems," "haptic," "scaled scores," "stanines"), or unnecessary complexity. Asking parents to share their particular expertise communicates respect as long as they perceive the request to be both legitimate and timely.
8. *Be there when needed.* If parents have a legitimate need to see the teacher, the teacher should do everything reasonable to meet them as soon as possible, even if it creates a slight inconvenience.

In addition to establishing a trusting relationship, the special educator will need to engage in specific tasks. They include attending the IEP conference, attending parent-teacher conferences, and developing ongoing communication. The remainder of this section will discuss each of these topics.

The IEP Conference

The purpose of this conference is to incorporate parental ideas into the student's educational program and to apprise parents of the teacher's focus for the year. The resource room teacher would be wise to consult with, or have present, regular classroom teachers who are involved with the student. Much can be done prior to, during, and after the conference to make parents feel that they are productive members of the team (McNamara, 1986).

Before the Conference. Before developing or updating the IEP, the teacher should schedule a group parent meeting. The major purpose of such a meeting is to explain the purpose of the IEP and to inform the parents of their legal rights. This meeting can also acquaint the parents with the format used by the school district. Letting parents know the rationale for the conference and the delivery of services provided for in the IEP will help to establish open lines of communication. Often parents sign the IEP signifying their approval of the program only to find that they are not receiving appropriate related services that are provided for under Public Law 94-142. Obviously, this situation does little to build up a trusting relationship between the home and the school. Being clear, precise, and up-front with the parents will pay high dividends in their ability to assist in carrying out the educational plan. Furthermore, it helps to allay any anxieties they may have regarding the parent-teacher conference.

If parents are going to be able to offer meaningful input in the IEP, they must have time to formulate their ideas. Coming into a meeting and being asked for suggestions cannot be considered "meaningful input." Teachers should send a letter to parents (see figure 15) at least two weeks prior to the conference requesting their ideas regarding the educational program of their child or adolescent. They should be provided with a stamped, addressed envelope. This lets them know that their input is important and valid and will be considered by the teacher. If parents do not respond to the letter, a phone call can be made in an attempt to get this important information.

Figure 15

Parent Information Form

Student: ______________________

Teacher: ______________________

Date: ______________________

On ____(fill in date)____ we will meet to develop or update the Individual Educational Plan for your child. Any ideas, thought, and concerns you have regarding the educational program for the year will be greatly appreciated. Feel free to use additional paper if necessary. Looking forward to seeing you.

Signed: ______________________

All of the above sets the stage for a productive meeting with parents.

During the Conference. Too often the school represents a threatening environment to parents of special children or adolescents. Teachers must do everything possible to make parents realize that they represent an integral component of their child's or adolescent's education. One suggestion is to have the meeting in a room other than the classroom. Classrooms are often filled with distracting stimuli, and rarely is there enough room for a table and three comfortable chairs. If the meeting must be in a classroom, the teacher should never sit behind the desk. This arrangement creates a physical, and perhaps psychological, barrier between the teacher and the parents. In addition, if any student's work is displayed, *all* of the student's work should be displayed. A circular table is preferred because no one is at the head and no one is therefore perceived as the most important or powerful. If at all possible, one should have refreshments available to add to the message that one is pleased to have the opportunity to plan this program with parents.

Just as parents come to these conferences with their preconceived notions, so do teachers. Teachers can (and should) explore their own attitudes and behaviors regarding parent-teacher conferences by completing the form "Are You a Teacher Who . . . ?" (see figure 16). This form can be adapted for each particular school and could be given to colleagues to enable them to explore their responses as a group. (See the Kroth & Simpon text for additional information).

If the IEP conference is to succeed, then special education teachers must be able to communicate in clear, precise language.

Unless teachers can transmit information to parents about the observable academic and social behaviors emitted by their children or adolescents, the time spent in teacher-parent interactions will be time ill spent. For example, rather than telling a parent that his or her child has an auditory comprehension deficit, the teacher should note that the child has difficulty understanding information when it is spoken. This kind of language provides a much more accurate description of students' strengths and weaknesses. As teachers, we tend to think that because we know the meaning of a term that the parent will also know it. However, teachers cannot assume that parents will understand their terminology. After all, why should they?

Teachers should also encourage parents to read all educational reports in great detail. Every unfamiliar word should be circled and discussed with the teacher. Parents should tape-record or take written notes. This practice not only provides them with a valuable record-keeping procedure that they can refer to at a later date, but also provides them with a glossary of unfamiliar terms. Finally, the most important suggestions is that teachers encourage parents to assert themselves. Parents should never feel embarrassed to ask a teacher what is meant by a technical term — it is their right to know (McNamara, 1979).

Figure 16

Are You A Teacher Who . . . ? (from Kroth and Simpon, 1977).

ALWAYS A	SOMETIMES B	NEVER C	
			1. never admits to a parent that you're wrong?
			2. has a sense of humor in a conference?
			3. lets parents smoke in a conference?
			4. serves coffee to parents during a conference?
			5. doesn't have any favorites?
			6. shows expression and emotions in a conference?
			7. shows expression and emotions in parent groups?
			8. starts conference or parent meetings on time?
			9. has contacts with parents?
			10. stops parent meetings at a scheduled time?
			11. has conferences in parents' homes?
			12. compares students with their older siblings?
			13. finds it hard to say "I don't know" to parents?
			14. talks less than 50 percent of each conference?
			15. talks about your own problems and solutions in conferences?
			16. sits behind a desk during conference?
			17. enjoys parent conferences?
			18. has examples of children's work to show parents?
			19. calls parents when things go well with their child?
			20. sends notes home when children have behavioral problems?
			21. uses grades to keep students in line?
			22. has ever had a principal sit in on one of your conferences?
			23. finds yourself criticizing more than praising your parents?
			24. has ever had dinner at a student's home?
			25. has ever had a parent over for dinner or a meeting at your home?

26. feels that parents have lost the respect of their children?
27. feels that parents have lost control of their children?
28. finds yourself physically drained at the end of a series of conferences?
29. has parent group meetings?
30. has strong negative feelings about certain racial or sexual groups?
31. prefers to have conferences with fathers rather than mothers?
32. studies a child's folder and past achievements before a conference?
33. argues with parents?
34. feels intimidated by parents?
35. demonstrates to parents effective ways to work with their child?
36. likes to problem-solve with parents?
37. involves parents in planning for their child??
38. encourages parents to visit class during class sessions?
39. uses parents as aides in the class?
40. does not want parents to teach their own children?
41. is honest with parents?
42. listens to parents?
43. dreads conference time?
44. has parents call on telephone to your home in the evening?
45. is positively reinforcing?
46. sends home daily report cards?
47. prepares handbooks or handouts for parents?
48. has good attendance at conference time or for group meetings?
49. has students sit in on conferences with their parents?
50. talks about other teachers to parents?

If possible, parents should receive a copy of the IEP at the completion of the conference. NCR (no carbon required) paper is especially helpful in this regard. Usually this is not possible with severely handicapped students because the sequence of skills is broken up into minute steps which invariably take up a great deal of paper. But this information should be sent to parents as soon as possible after they have approved the plan.

After the Conference. Parents should be provided with an opportunity to evaluate the IEP conference. This practice has the advantage of providing the teacher with systematic feedback that he or she can use to improve performance and to better meet parental needs. The form developed by Hudson and Graham, 1978 (see figure 17) is excellent for this purpose. As the authors note, the form can be adapted for individual school district needs; however, the philosophical intent of parent participation must be maintained.

Figure 17

Parent Form for Staffing Conference Feedback (from Hudson and Graham, 1978, pp. 309-318).

Student ______________________ Date ______________

School ______________________ Grade ______________

Parent(s) ______________________ Telephone ______________

Home address ______________________________________

Staffing date ______________________ Time ______________

Parents attending staffing conference ______________________

____

____

To The Parent: The purpose of this questionnaire is to obtain information that will assist the Special Service Staff in improving communication between parents and professionals.

Recently you participated in a staffing conference concerning your child's needs. Based on your feelings about the conference please respond to the following questions. For each question, check either "yes," "partially," or "no." If you wish to provide additional information please print your statement. The last three questions are open-ended; therefore, you may respond to them with a written statement.

I. **Administrative**

A. Were you notified that you child had been referred for special education services prior to your invitation to attend the staffing conference? ( ) yes ( ) partially ( ) no

B. Was an effort made to have both parents participate in the staffing conference? ( ) yes ( ) partially ( ) no

C. Were you notified of the staffing conference early enough to ensure your participation? ( ) yes ( ) partially ( ) no

D. Was the staffing conference scheduled at a mutually agreed-upon time and place? ( ) yes ( ) partially ( ) no

E. Were you told who would be attending the staffing conference? ( ) yes ( ) partially ( ) no

F. Were you informed of the purpose of the staffing conference? ( ) yes ( ) partially ( ) no

G. Were you told that you could invite outside professionals retained by you? ( ) yes ( ) partially ( ) no

H. Were you informed of due process procedures and your rights to appeal decisions? ( ) yes ( ) partially ( ) no

I. Were you provided a copy of the IEP? ( ) yes ( ) partially ( ) no

II. **Profesional**

A. Were team members knowledgeable of your child's emotional and social behavior? ( ) yes ( ) partially ( ) no

B. Were team members knowledgeable of your child's academic status? ( ) yes ( ) partially ( ) no

C. Was a variety of service options discussed relative to your child's needs? ( ) yes ( ) partially ( ) no

D. Was the assessment information collected from a variety of sources? ( ) yes ( ) partially ( ) no

E. Was the assessment evaluation conducted by a multidisciplinary team? ( ) yes ( ) partially ( ) no

F. Do you feel that the test instruments used were culturally or racially discriminatory? ( ) yes ( ) partially ( ) no

G. Did the team justify any removal of your child from the regular classroom? ( ) yes ( ) partially ( ) no

III. **Parental**

A. Did you feel comfortable attending the staffing conference? ( ) yes ( ) partially ( ) no

B. Were you asked about your opinions? ( ) yes ( ) partially ( ) no

C. Did you feel free to contribute suggestions regarding your child's needs? ( ) yes ( ) partially ( ) no

D. Did the professional staff appear interested in what you had to say? ( ) yes ( ) partially ( ) no

E. Do you feel that the professional staff felt your participation was important? ( ) yes ( ) partially ( ) no

F. Were you provided ample time to express information that you felt to be relevant? ( ) yes ( ) partially ( ) no

G. Did you understand the IEP developed for your child? ( ) yes ( ) partially ( ) no

H. Did you feel that your child should have participated in the staffing conference? ( ) yes ( ) partially ( ) no

IV. **General**

A. Do you feel that the recommendations made were in the best interest of your child? ( ) yes ( ) partially ( ) no

B. Are you satisfied with the decision made at the staffing conference? ( ) yes ( ) partially ( ) no

C. Do you feel that support services other than those recommended are needed for your child's progress? ( ) yes ( ) partially ( ) no

D. Did you feel free to ask questions regarding the contributions, evaluation, and suggestions of the

1. classroom teacher? ( ) yes ( ) partially ( ) no
2. Learning specialist or special teacher? ( ) yes ( ) partially ( ) no
3. special education representative or administration? ( ) yes ( ) partially ( ) no
4. assessment team member? ( ) yes ( ) partially ( ) no
5. school psychologist? ( ) yes ( ) partially ( ) no
6. ____________________? ( ) yes ( ) partially ( ) no

E. At the conclusion of the staffing conference, how did you perceive your child's problems in view of your previous understanding?

____

____

____

____

F. Remarks

____

____

Parent-Teacher Conferences

The IEP conference should be viewed as the beginning of the communication process, not the end. The goal should be to increase parental involvement prior to the IEP conference, to communicate effectively during the conference, and to provide parents with opportunities to meet and talk throughout the school year. One way to provide these opportunities is to attend the traditional parent-teacher conferences. Much of what was stated above is applicable here. A few other tips are offered by the editors of *Academic Therapy* (1987, pp. 411-412):

- Mail a written note (it's better not to trust Johnny to deliver it) or call the parents to establish a firm conference date. When so many mothers are working outside of the home, setting a time during the school day may be difficult. If so, check with your principal or district to determine policies on after school or evening conferences.
- Request a confirmation of the time, place, and date if you have used a written, mailed communication. (Nothing beats a *mailed* note over and beyond a telephone call.)
- Read the student's cumulative folder thoroughly. Be familiar with the vast array of tests that have been administered to the child. Doublecheck. Are there any gaps that require updated testing in specific areas, e.g., math, oral reading, et cetera? If so, determine who will do the testing and when. You will need that information prior to your appointment with the parents.
- In addition to test results, set aside a folder showing school assignments from September through the conference date. Point out the ways in which these illustrate the student's strengths and weaknesses.
- Be positive. Start the conference with a description of an area in which the child has excelled. Then move into ongoing needs.
- A desk can become a barrier. Try to sit in a cluster, for example, around a utility table, so that test results and work samples can be comfortably shared. Keep your language simple and nontechnical. It is a kindness to say to parents, "Please interrupt me if any time I should use a term or make a statement that you do not understand."
- The conference should be a two-way dialogue. Engage the parents as much as possible. Get their observations on how Johnny and Susan react to school, learning, homework, friends. Listen! Be sure to let them know how much you value their opinions. Parents

have much to offer and sometimes need to be reassured of the contribution they make to the youngster's well-being.

— When possible, have the child participate in the school conference in keeping with the mandates of PL94-142.

— A conference should not last longer than one hour. Allow time to summarize and make recommendations for the coming year as well as suggestions for summer activities.

— If the physical set-up makes it possible, a cup of coffee sets a warm, friendly tone.

Kroth (1985, p. 73) cites a conference checklist developed by the Parent Center in Albuquerque, New Mexico, that can be another useful way to prepare for the conference.

Preconference

________ 1. Notify
- purpose, place, time, length of time allotted

________ 2. Prepare
- review child's folder
- gather examples of work
- prepare materials

________ 3. Plan agenda

________ 4. Arrange environment
- comfortable seating
- eliminate distractions

Conference

________ 1. Welcome
- establish rapport

________ 2. State
- purpose
- time limitations
- note taking
- options for follow-up

________ 3. Encourage
- information sharing
- comments
- questions

________ 4. Listen
- pause once in a while!
- look for verbal and nonverbal cues
- questions

________ 5 Summarize
(End on positive note!)

Postconference

________ 1. Review conference with child, if appropriate.

________ 2. Share information with other school personnel, if needed.

________ 2. Mark calendar for planned follow-up.

Ongoing Activities

In addition to the activities noted above, resource room teachers should develop ongoing activities that will enable them and the parents to keep in touch. They may include the following:

Periodic phone calls (focus on the positive)

Periodic notes to parents (again, try to be positive)

Monthly meetings

Home-school reinforcement systems (see Kroth, 1985, for specific details)

Breakfast meetings prior to school for working parents who may be overscheduled during the evening

Parents' Perceptions of Resource Room Teachers

An informal, nonscientific survey of parents of students who attend resource rooms revealed that their expections of the resource room teacher are very high. They see this person as an "expert" who can remediate a wide variety of disabilities in just about every school subject. Beyond this, they appear to view the resource room teacher as someone who is really "looking out for" their child: someone who acts as a liaison between the student and the regular classroom teacher, someone who is concerned about the child's social and emotional needs, as well as his or her academic performance. It may well be asking a great deal of one person to do all of this, yet it appears that many are capable of and willing to take on these responsibilities. It is hoped that the information provided herein will facilitate this task.

References

Alberto, P.A., and Troutman, A.C. (1982). *Applied behavior analysis for teachers.* Columbus, Ohio: Chas. E. Merrill.

Alley, G., and Deshler, D. (1979). *Teaching the learning disabled adolescent: Strategies and methods.* Denver: Love Publishing.

Anderson-Inman, L. (1986). Bridging the gap: Student-generated strategies for promoting the transfer of learning. *Exceptional Children, 52,* 562-572.

Blankenship, C., and Lilly, S. (1981). *Mainstreaming students with learning and behavior problems.* New York: Holt, Rinehart and Winston.

Bornstein, P., and Lauber, E. (1986). *Resource room manual.* Harborfields Central School District, Greenlawn, N.Y.

Brown, R., and Elliott, R. (1965). Control of aggression in a nursery school class. *Journal of Experimental Child Psychology, 2,* 103-107.

Brown, V. (1975). A basic Q-sheet for analyzing and comparing curriculum materials and proposals. *Journal of Learning Disabilities*, *8*, 7, 409-410.

Bruner, J. (1966) *Toward a theory of instruction.* Cambridge, Mass.: Belknap Press of Harvard University.

Bucher, B., and King, L.W. (1971). Generalization of punishment effect in the deviant behavior of a psychotic child. *Behavior Therapy*, *2*, 68-71.

Bushell, D. (1973) The behavior analysis classroom. In B. Spodek (Ed.), *Early Childhood Education.* Englewood Cliffs, N.J.: Prentice Hall.

Calkins, L. McC. (1986). *The art of teaching writing*. Portsmouth, N.H.: Heinemann.

Cartledge, G., and Milburn, J.F. (Eds.) (1980). *Teaching social skills to children*. New York: Pergamon.

Cienion, M. (1968). Some aspects of a learning-resource room. In J.I. Arena (Ed.), *Successful programming: Many points of view*. Pittsburgh, Pa.: Association for Children with Learning Disabilities.

Cohen, S.B., and Safran, J. (1981). A conference training model for learning disabled resource teachers. *Learning Disability Quarterly, 4*, 302-306.

Deno, S., and Merkin, P. (1977). *Data-based program modification*. Reston, Va.: C.E.C. Publications.

__________. (1980). Data-based IEP development: An approach to substantive compliance. *Teaching Exceptional Children, 12*, 92-98.

Deshler, D., and Schumacher, J.B. (1986). Learning strategies: An instructional alternative for low achieving adolescents. *Exceptional Children, 52*, 583-589.

Drabman, R.S. and Lahey, B.B. (1974). Feedback in classroom behavior modification: Effects on the target and her classrmates. *Journal of Applied Behavior Analysis, 7*, 591-598.

Dunn, Lloyd M. (1968). Special education for mildly retarded: Is much of it justified? *Exceptional Children, 35*, 5-22.

Editorial Staff (1987). Parent-teacher conferences: The professional's point of view. *Academic Therapy, 24*, 411-412.

Ferritor, D.E., Buchholdt, D., Hamblin, R.L., and Smith, L. (1972). The non-effects of contingency reinforcement for attending behavior on work accomplished. *Journal of Applied Behavior Analysis, 5*, 7-17.

Friend, M., and McNutt, G. (1984). Resource room programs: Where are we now? *Exceptional Children, 51*, 150-155.

Fry, E.B. (1977). *Elementary reading instruction*. New York: McGraw-Hill.

Gardner, J.M. (1972). Teaching behavior modification to nonprofessionals. *Journal of Applied Behavior Analysis, 5*, 517-521.

Gearheart, B.R. (1985). *Learning disabilities: Educational strategies*. 4th Edition. St. Louis, Mo.: Times Mirror/Mosby College Publications.

Glass, G.V. (1983). Effectiveness of special education. *Policy Studies Review, 2*, Special #1, 65-78.

Goldstein, A.P., Sprafkin, R.P., Gershaw, N.J., and Klein, P. (1980). *Skillstreaming the adolescent: A structured learning approach to teaching prosocial skills.* Champaign, Ill.: Research Press.

Graham, S., and Miller, L. (1979). Spelling research and practice: A unified approach. *Focus on Exception Children, 11*, 2.

———. (1980). Handwriting remediation and principles: A unified approach. *Focus on Exceptional Children, 12*, 2.

Graves, D.H. (1983) *Writing: Teachers and children at work.* Portsmouth, N.H.: Heinemann.

Greer, R.D., and Dorow, L.G. (1976). *Specializing education behaviorally: A data-based approach for teachers in special education.* Dubuque, Iowa: Kendall/Hunt.

Hall, R.V. (1971). *Managing behavior.* Lawrence, Kans.: H & H Enterprises.

Hall, R.V., Fox, R., Willard, D., Goldsmith, L., Emerson, M., Owen, M., Davis, F., and Porcia, F. (1971). The teacher as observer and experimenter in the modification of disputing and talking out behavior. *Journal of Applied Behavior Analysis, 4*, 141-149.

Hallahan, D.P., and Kauffman, J. (1976). *Introduction to learning disabilities: A psycho-behavioral approach.* Englewood Cliffs, N.J.: Prentice-Hall.

Hallerick, R.L. (1969). The creative learning center. *Elementary School Journal, 69*, 259-264.

Hammill, D.D. (1972). The resource room model in special education. *The Journal of Special Education, 6*, 349-354.

Hammill, D.D., and Bartel, N.R. (Eds.) (1971). *Educational perspectives in learning disability.* New York: John Wiley.

Hanser, S.B. (1973). *Group contingent music listening in emotionally disturbed boys.* Paper presented to the 24th annual convention of the National Association for Music Therapy, Athens, Ga.

Harris, F.R., Johnson, M., Kelley, C.S., and Wolf, M.M. (1966). Effects of positive social reinforcement on regressed crawling of a nursery school child. *Journal of Educational Psychology, 55*, 35-41.

Hawkins, R.P., Peterson, R.K., Schweid, E., and Bijou, S. (1966). Behavior therapy in the home: Amelioration of problem parent-child relations with the parent in a therapeutic role. *Journal of Experimental Child Psychology, 4*, 99-107.

Hewitt, F. (1968). *The emotionally disturbed child in the classroom.* Boston: Allyn and Bacon.

Holms, D.S. (1966). The application of learning theory in the treatment of a school behavior problem: A case study. *Psychology in the Schools, 3*, 355-358.

Homme, C. (1970). *How to use contingency contracts in the classroom.* Champaign, Ill.: Research Press.

Hopins, B.L., and Conard, R.V. (1976). Putting it all together: Super school. In Haring and R. Schiefelbusch *Teaching exceptional children.* New York: McGraw-Hill.

Howell, K.W., and Morehead, M.K. (1987). *Currciulum-based evaluation for special and remedial education.* Columbus, Ohio: Chas. E. Merrill.

Hudson, F.G., and Graham, S. (1978). An approach to operationalizing the IEP *Learning Disabilities Quarterly, 1*, 13-32.

Isaacson, S. (1988). Teaching written expression. *Teaching Exceptional Children, 20*, 32-33.

Jenkins, J.R., and Mayhall, W.F. (1976). Development and evaluation of a resource teacher program. *Exceptional Children, 43*, 21-30.

Johnson, D.J., and Myklebust, H.R. (1967). Learning disabilities: Educational principles and practices. New York: Grune and Stratton.

Johnson, G. Orville (1962). Special education for the mentally handicapped. *Exceptional Children, 29*, 62-69.

Kalish, H.I. (1981) *From behavioral science to behvior modification.* New York: McGraw-Hill.

Kazdin, A.E. (1973). The effects of vicarious reinforcement on attending behavior in the classroom. *Journal of Applied Behavior Analysis, 6*, 71-78.

Kazdin, A.E. (1982). The token economy: A decade later. *Journal of Applied Behavior Analysis, 15*, 431-445.

Kelly, E.L. (1979). *Elementary school social studies instruction: A basic approach.* Denver: Love Publishing.

Koegal, R.L., and Covert, A. (1972). The relationship of self-stimulation to learning in autistic children. *Journal of Applied Behavior Analysis, 5*, 381-387.

Kroth, R.L. (1985). *Communicating with parents of exceptional children.* 2nd Edition. Denver, Colo.: Love Publishing.

Kroth, R.L., and Simpson, R.L. (1977). *Parent conferences as a teaching strategy.* Denver, Colo.: Love Publishing.

Larsen, S.C., and Poplin, M.S. (1980). *Methods for educating the handicapped: An individualized education program approach.* Boston: Allyn and Bacon.

McDaniel, T.R. (1986). A primer on classroom discipline: Principles old and new. *Phi Delta Kappan*, Sept., 63-67.

McLoughlin, J.A., and Remer, R. (1983). Urban resource teachers and their needs. *Learning Disability Quarterly, 6*, 349-352.

MacMillan, Donald L. (1971). Special education for the mildly retarded: Servant or savant. *Focus on Exceptional Children, 2*, 1-11.

McNamara, B.E. (1977). *The effect of instruction in principles of learning and techniques of teaching versus techniques of teaching on teachers' social reinforcement behavior.* Doctural dissertation, Teachers College, Columbia University.

__________. (1979). Talk without "teacherese." *Academic Therapy, 15*, 227-230.

__________. (1981). Communicating effectively with regular educators. *The Forum*, Spring, 20-22.

__________. (1985). Teacher consultation: The key to a successful resource room program. *Perceptions*, Summer, 5.

__________. (1986). Parents as partners in the I.E.P. process. *Academic Therapy, 21*, 309-319.

Madsen, C.K., and Forsythe, J.L. (1974). The effect of contingent music on increases of mathematical responses. In C.K. Madsen, R.D. Greer, and C.H. Madsen (Eds.), *Research in music behavior.* New York: Teachers College Press.

Madsen, C.H., and Madsen, C.K. (1974). *Teaching/discipline: A positive approach for educational development.* Expanded Second Edition for Professionals. Boston: Allyn and Bacon.

__________. (1981). *Teaching/discipline: A positive approach for educational development.* 3rd Edition. Boston: Allyn and Bacon.

Margolis, H., and Brannigan, G.G. (1986). Building trust with parents. *Academic Therapy, 22*, 1, 71-74.

Mercer, C.D., and Mercer, A.R. (1985). *Teaching students with learning problems.* 2nd Edition. Columbus, Ohio: Chas. E. Merrill.

Murray, D.M. (1982). *Living by teaching.* Upper Montclair, N.J.: Boynton/Cook Publishers.

Myers, P., and Hammill, D.D. (1976). *Methods for learning disorders.* 2nd Edition. New York: John Wiley.

O'Leary, S.G., and O'Leary, K.D. (1976). Behavior modification in the school. In H. Leitenberg (Ed.), *Handbook of behavior modification.* Englewood Cliffs, N.J.: Prentice-Hall.

Palincsar, A.S. (1986). Metacognitive strategy instruction. *Exceptional Children, 53*, 118-124.

Parsonson, B., Baer, A., and Baer, D. (1974). The application of generalized correct social contingencies: An evaluation of a training program. *Journal of Applied Behavior Analysis, 7*, 427-437.

Pertsh, C.F. (1936). A comparative study of the progress of subnormal pupils in the grades and in special classes. Doctoral dissertation, Teachers College, Columbia University.

Polloway, E.A., and Cohen, S.B. (1981). Written language for the mildly handicapped student. *Focus on Exceptional Children, 14*, 3.

Reger, R. (1969). *Resource room program: Outline and concept. Erie County, N.Y., BOCES 1.*

__________. (1972). *Resource rooms: Change agents or guardians of the status quo? The Journal of Special Education, 6*, 355-359.

__________. (1973). What is a resource room program? *Journal of Learning Disabilities, 6*, 607-614.

Reiter, D. (1986). The role of the resource room teacher. Master's thesis, Hofstra University.

Reynolds, M.C., and Birch, J.W. (1977). *Teaching exceptional children in America's schools.* Reston, Va.: C.E.C. Publications.

Reynolds, M.C., Wang, M.C., and Walberg, H.J. (1987). The necessary restructuring of special and regular education. *Exceptional Children, 53*, 391-398.

Sabatino, D.A. (1972). Resource rooms: The renaissance in special education. *The Journal of Special Education, 6*, 335-347.

Salvia, J., and Ysseldyke, J.E. (1983). *Assessment in special and remedial education.* 2nd Edition. Boston: Houghton Mifflin.

Thurlow, M.L., Ysseldyke, J.E., Grader, J.L., and Algozzine, B. (1983). What's special about the special education resource room for the learning disabled student? *Learning Disability Quarterly, 6*, 283-288.

Shattuck, Marchis. (1946). Segregation versus non-segregation of exceptional children. *Journal of Exceptional Children, 12*, 235-240.

Shulene, J.A. (1975). Question: When is a picture a riddle? Answer: When the riddle is the picture! *Teaching Exceptional Children, 7*, 68-70.

Shutte, R., and Hopkins, B.L. (1970). The effects of teacher attention on following instructions in a kindergarten class. *Journal of Applied Behavior Analysis, 3*, 117-122.

Siegal, E., and Gold, R. (1982). *Educating the learning disabled.* New York: Macmillan.

Silverman, R., Zigmond, N., and Sanzone, J. (1981). Teaching coping skills to adolescents with learning problems. *Focus on Exceptional Children, 13*, February.

Smith, C.R. (1983). *Learning disabilities: The interaction of learner, task, and setting.* Boston: Little, Brown.

Speece, D.L., and Mandell, C.J. (1980). Resource room support services for regular teachers. *Learning Disabilities Quarterly, 3*, 1, 49-53.

Stephens, T.M., and Cooper, J.O. (1980). The token economy: An affirmative perspective. *The Educational Forum*, November, 107-111.

Stowitschek, J.J., Gable, R.A., and Hendrickson, J.M. (1980). *Instructional materials for exceptional children: Selection, management and adaptation.* Germantown, Maryland: An Aspen Publication.

Strauss, A.A., and Kephart, N.C. (1955). *Psychopathology and education of the brain injured child, Vol. 2., Progress in theory and clinic.* New York: Grune and Stratton.

Suffolk County, N.Y., BOCES 2 (1986). The Resource Room Standards Committee.

Tate, B.G., and Baroff, G.S. (1966). Aversive control of self-injurious behavior in a psychotic boy. *Behavior Research and Therapy, 4*, 281-287.

Taylor, R. (1984). *Assessment of exceptional students: Educational and psychological procedures.* Springfield, Ill.: Chas. Thomas Publishers.

Thomas, D.R., Becker, W.C., and Armstrong, M. (1968). Production and elimination of descriptive behavior by systematically varying teachers' behavior. *Journal of Applied Behavior Analysis, 1*, 3-45.

Thurlow, M.L., Ysseldyke, J.E. (1983). *Assessment in special and remedial eduaction.* 2nd Edition. Boston: Houghton Mifflin.

Tucker, J.A. (1985). Curriculum-based assessment: An introduction. *Exceptional Children, 52*, 3, 199-204.

Van Etten C., and Adamson, G. (1973). The fail-save program: A special education continuum. *Instructional Alternatives for Exceptional Children.* Council for Exceptional Children, Reston, Virginia: 156-165.

Watson, B., and Van Etten, C. (1976). Material analysis. *Journal of Learning Disabilities, 9*, 13-17.

Weiss, H.G., and Weiss, M.S. (1974). *A survival manual: Case studies and suggestions for the learning disabled teenager.* Great Barrington, Mass.: Treehouse Associates.

White, M.A. (1975). Natural roles of teacher approval and disapproval in the classroom. *Journal of Applied Behavior Analysis, 8*, 367-372.

Wiederholt, L., Hammill, D.D., and Brown, V. (1983). *The resource room teacher.* 2nd Edition. Boston,: Allyn and Bacon.

Will, M.C. (1986). Educating children with learning problems: A shared responsibility. *Exceptional Children, 52*, 411-416.

Ypseldyke, J.E., and Algozzine, B. (1983). L.D. or not L.D.: That's not the question. *Journal of Learning Disabilities, 16*, 29-31.

Zigmond, N., Vallecorsa, A., and Silverman, R. (1983). *Assessment for instructional planning in special education.* Englewood Cliffs, N.J.: Prentice-Hall.

Index